It happened in
SHROPSHIRE

Bob Burrows

Merlin Unwin Books

First published in Great Britain by Merlin Unwin Books, 2010
Text © Bob Burrows, 2010

Published by:
Merlin Unwin Books Ltd
Palmers House
7 Corve Street
Ludlow
Shropshire SY8 1DB
U.K.

www.merlinunwin.co.uk

The author asserts his moral right to be identified with this work.
Designed and set in Bembo by Hannah McMillan
Printed in Great Britain by Cromwell Press Group

ISBN 978 1 906122 19 5

BOB BURROWS is a retired Area Director of Lloyds TSB Bank who took up writing as a hobby in 2001. To date he has had almost 100 articles published in magazines and newspapers. *It Happened in Shropshire* is his eighth book. His first, *Fighter Writer*, the biography of a First World War poet, was launched at the Imperial War Museum in London and he was nominated for the Saltire Award in two categories. Married to Pat, a proud father of two and an even prouder grandfather of two, he is a sports fanatic.

CONTENTS

To the pots of gold at the end of my rainbow:

Emily Grace Burrows
born 30 April 2004

Jacob Alexander Lynes Bates
born 10 May 2008

THE COUNTY OF SHROPSHIRE

Ellesmere ●

Market Drayton
Styche Hall

● Oswestry

● Wem

🏌 *Llanymynech Golf Club*

🏌 *Hawkstone Park*

⚔ *battlefield*

● SHREWSBURY

● Telford

⛏ Lead mines
Stiperstones

🦅 *Wroxeter*

Ironbridge

✝ Ratlinghope

● Much Wenlock
⬤⬤⬤⬤⬤

Long Mynd

Caer Caradoc

● Church Stretton

● Bridgnorth

● Bishops Castle

● Craven Arms

Clun ●

Heath House

Stanton Lacy ✝

Cleobury Mortimer ●

● Ludlow

INTRODUCTION

Shropshire is a unique part of the British Isles in so many ways. Until King Offa of Mercia annexed the area in the 8th century, Shropshire was part of Wales and for centuries became a buffer between Wales and England and a political pawn, as successive invaders battled over its domain.

The Romans, Saxons, Vikings, Danes and the Normans have all in some way left their mark on this beautiful part of these islands.

It Happened In Shropshire is intended to entertain and to give a snapshot, a full-colour snapshot, of Shropshire, its Salopian citizens, events both historical and mythical and its development – while also attempting to highlight the county's contribution to Britain's history and culture.

Perversely the scholar and poet renowned for singing the praises of Shropshire was neither born, raised, educated nor lived in the county but has become synonymous with Shropshire through his poem, *A Shropshire Lad*. Alfred Edward Housman wrote several of his poems about Shropshire without having set foot in the county. His 'blue remembered hills' were his view of the Shropshire hills from a hilltop in his hometown of Fockbury, Worcestershire. The majority of his time was spent in London where he was Professor

6

of Latin at University College before being appointed Kennedy Professor of Latin at Cambridge in 1911.

His acclaimed work, *A Shropshire Lad*, is written from the perspective of a young man living in London, feeling lonely and nostalgic for his home county and his past. When the book of poetry was published and became successful, those who knew Housman personally had difficulty reconciling his sober, almost severe presence, with the whimsical, nostalgic first person of his poetry sequence. Furthermore, those who came to Shropshire seeking the places that Housman featured in his work were often confounded to find that he had changed certain features. Nevertheless he did visit Shropshire from time to time and when he died in 1936 his ashes were buried outside the north wall of St Laurence's Church in Ludlow, where now a tablet is inscribed with a few lines of his poetry.

Before embarking on the task of constructing this book I had what best could be described as a skimpy knowledge of the county.

A. E. Housman's memorial,
St Laurence's Church, Ludlow.
The lines of poetry read:
'Goodnight ensured release,
Imperishable Peace,
Have these for yours.'

However, after research and visiting many parts of Shropshire, I must confess that I now share Housman's love of the county. The countryside and the picturesque, unspoilt villages and towns are best characterised, I think, by the small town of Much Wenlock where I stayed.

There I encountered no graffiti, local people comfortable with one another, an excellent programme of community events and a real sense of community spirit. Superb medieval buildings, the Guild Hall dating from 1540, the Priory ruins going back to the 12th century and the timbered 1682 Raynald's Mansion in the High Street are complemented by the up-to-date service at the *Raven Hotel*. Built in 1700, the hotel incorporates Alms Houses from the 15th century and in the grounds are the remnants of a hall from the 14th century. Inside the hotel, the dining rooms are linked by a conservatory, the tiled floor of which has embedded in it a round toughened glass aperture, affording a glimpse into an ancient well below.

Baron De Coubertin was staying in Much Wenlock in 1890 when he addressed a meeting of 60 local people at *The Raven*. He had come to the town to meet William Penny Brookes, founder of the Modern Olympic Games. The hotel represents all that is best in my experience of Shropshire, utilising the history of the town to attract visitors and then by good service and cuisine that compares favourably with a top restaurant, ensuring that the visitor will want to return.

Many excellent books have been written by experts in their field on the history of Shropshire, its geology, canals, railways, mines, murders, its myths and legends. During my research I have been very much entertained and in awe of the authors' detailed knowledge in their specialised fields. I cannot hope to replicate in one book the fine detail of so many expert publications in so many specialised subjects.

Nevertheless, I trust that readers will be able to dip in and out of this publication, seeking those pieces that interest them, and I hope that by avoiding too much detail and by keeping the narrative flowing, this book will have appeal to most Salopians and to those with a genuine interest in the county's history, characters and evolution.

Salopians! What are the origins of this term which refers to a native of Shropshire? The Normans had a word for the area that was so unpronounceable that they shortened and softened it to Salopesberia or Salopescira and naturally, over the centuries, it softened to Salop. In 1888 the county council was actually called Salop County Council, a title that formally lasted until 1980 when the name of Shropshire County Council was adopted. However, a native of Shropshire is still today referred to as a Salopian.

The medieval High Street in Much Wenlock is flanked by glorious timber-framed buildings, limestone cottages and Elizabethan architecture.

NOT MANY PEOPLE KNOW THIS!
UNIQUE SHROPSHIRE FACTS

1. The River Severn is the longest river in Britain. It was once also the busiest river in Europe.

2. Charles II famously hid from Roundhead soldiers in an oak tree in the grounds of Boscobel House, near Albrighton, in 1651.

3. In 1709, Abraham Darby became the first man to use coal in the form of coke in the process of iron smelting.

4. The world's first cast iron bridge was built in Ironbridge in 1779 by Darby's grandson, Abraham Darby III.

5. The Ironbridge Gorge Museum is now a World Heritage Site.

6. Lord Hill of Hawkstone Park was second-in-command to Wellington at the Battle of Waterloo in 1815.

7. The modern Olympic Games were born in Much Wenlock in 1850.

8. Shrewsbury MP Benjamin Disraeli became Prime Minister in 1868 and again in 1874 for a further 6 years.

9. Shrewsbury Flower Show was established in 1875. It is the oldest in the world.

10. Also in 1875, Dawley-born Matthew Webb became the first man to successfully swim the English Channel.

11. In 1911, Whitchurch-born composer Edward German wrote a *Coronation March and Hymn* for King George V.

12. During World War II, General Charles de Gaulle and his family were offered sanctuary in Gadlas Hall, Ellesmere, from 1940-1.

13. League soccer came to Shrewsbury, Shropshire in 1950.

14. Salopian Sir Gordon Richards was knighted in 1953. He remains the only jockey to receive a Knighthood.

15. In April 1959, footballer Billy Wright became the first player to win 100 caps for the English national side.

16. The 1966 World Cup-winning England football team trained at Lilleshall Sports Centre.

17. Shrewsbury won the popular television programme *It's a Knockout* in 1969.

18. Telford United Football Club played in the very first non-League F.A. Cup Final at Wembley in 1970.

19. The lowest-ever weather temperature was recorded on 10 January, 1982 in Edgmond, Telford. The temperature was -26°C.

20. The 1987 Golf World Matchplay final was contested by two Salopians: Ian Woosnam and Sandy Lyle.

21. Both Woosnam and Lyle won the US Masters at Augusta National Golf Club in 1988 and 1991 respectively.

22. The G8 Summit of World Leaders was held at Weston Park in 1998.

23. Bridgnorth has the only inland cliff railway in Britain.

24. Shrewsbury is considered to be one of the most haunted towns in Britain.

Chapter One

SHROPSHIRE: A PROFILE

Shropshire has under 300,000 inhabitants spread across its 1,250 square miles, so it is not densely populated, that ratio being only a third of the national average. For its size though, Shropshire has made an astonishing contribution to England's social and cultural history.

To most people the county is best known for its medieval towns and castles, for being close to the Welsh Border, for the wonder and ingenuity of Offa's Dyke, for being the birthplace of the Industrial Revolution, and for its farming. However, it has also produced some remarkable individuals who have represented Britain on the world stage and Shropshire has, over the centuries, remained vibrant and has used the advantages of its geography and history to good effect.

Britain, over the millennia, has been submerged under tropical warm waters, frozen in the Ice Age, turned to barren desert, and covered in huge rain forests. Shropshire of course has undergone the same cycle and much of the county was fashioned by forces beyond the control of man. Amazing to think that Wenlock Edge was once under warm tropical waters and when it rose up out of the sea it was formed out of millions and millions of shells of small marine life forms.

More than 300 million years ago large parts of Shropshire were under tropical warm swamps, containing giant ferns and rotting trees and vegetation that were gradually absorbed into the stagnating swamp, mud and moisture. As time moved on, the residue formed peat which in turn became compressed and solidified into coal. These layers were eventually exposed to water brought down by rivers containing limestone from the shells of millions of small sea creatures.

The rich geological layers would, millions of years later, form the foundation of Shropshire's Industrial Revolution. The geological cycle resulted in the formation of seams of coal, limestone and iron-laden rock, the raw materials so crucial to the smelting of iron, which was to be the springboard of Shropshire's industrial boom. **The planet Earth embraces 12 recognised geological phases – Shropshire bears the evidence of 10 of them!**

One of the very first inhabitants of the county has been traced back as far as the Triassic Period, around 240 million years ago. Its fossils indicate that the plant-eating reptile, Rynchosaurus, had the capability of growing to the size of a small hippopotamus, and its footprints have been found in the quarry at Grinshill, Shropshire.

However, evidence of a more exotic Shropshire resident, dating from the Ice Age, was discovered by a lady whose dog started to dig in a gravel pit in a quarry in the village of Condover in September 1986. Subsequent excavations revealed the exciting discovery of the remains of five Woolly Mammoths: one adult and four juveniles. The skeleton of the adult is believed to be the most complete of any Woolly Mammoth found in Great Britain. In 2009 scientists form the Natural History Museum in London, following state-of-the-art radiocarbon dating technology, established that the animals had died around 14,000 years ago. It had previously been believed that the Woolly Mammoth became extinct in north-west Europe more than 20,000 years ago. The Shropshire find was important in that it confirmed that mammoths had survived in

Britain for much longer than previously accepted.

In May 2009 staff at the Orthopaedic Hospital at Gobowen, north Shropshire, at the request of the Ludlow Museum Resource Centre who supplied bones from the adult mammoth, were requested to X-ray the remains to ascertain the cause of death. Daniel Lockett, the curator of natural science at the Ludlow Museum Resource Centre which proudly houses more than 80% of the original find, told me in November 2009 that the results of the cause of death were still being analysed. There is a model of the adult mammoth taken from the original skeleton, on display at the Shropshire Hills Discovery Centre in Craven Arms.

The Ice Age 15,000 years ago was responsible for geographically shaping the Shropshire of today. As the huge glaciers covering the landscape started to thaw and move, massive channels were gouged out of the land. As the ice retreated it created valleys and ravines and a rich mix of clay and sand, the Shropshire soil that would much later form the basis of its agricultural industry. The melting ice bore with it boulders, rocks and other abrasive materials, sandpapering landscapes smooth of any protruding features. Sometimes the ice sheets caused the softer muddier ground to cave in and resulted in the formation of lakes.

The consequence of nature's volatility resulted in Shropshire being fashioned into two distinct areas. The north of the county has a large, flat, fertile plain and is plentiful in sandstone left over from the days when the region was covered by desert. Most of Shropshire's larger towns are located in the north. The south of the county is very different, with hill ranges, river valleys, forests and woods.

Here, an area of some 300 square miles is designated as an area of Outstanding Natural Beauty. It was eulogised by the Shropshire poet A. E. Housman. The county's distinctive natural geographical features include Ironbridge Gorge, the distinctive Long Mynd plateau at 1760 feet high and the jagged, bleak Stiperstones at 1690 feet high. Brown Clee Hill, one of the Clee Hills range, is the highest of all at 1790 feet. Most of the county is more rural, sparsely populated, well-forested and very much a creation of those very early, violent forces of nature.

Ancient tools, mainly flints made from pebbles or shards of rock, indicate that Man inhabited the Shropshire area around 4000BC. Neolithic arrowheads and stone axes indicate activity during the latter stages of the Stone Age and there is plentiful evidence of Shropshire life around the Bronze Age. Burial mounds at Long Mynd, Shrewsbury and Ludlow, stone circles, dug-out canoes and evidence of trade with flints identified as having come from East Anglia in exchange for stone axes, indicate an active, thriving community.

However, there is plenty of evidence throughout the county of fortified settlements of round huts and hill forts through the Stone Age, Bronze Age and Iron Age to indicate that it was also a violent time when ancient man was forced to protect his crops, animals, fishing ground and family.

Shropshire has benefited from exposure to a series of cultures from totally different environments: the Welsh border tribes, followed by the Romans, Saxons, Vikings and then the Normans have all left distinctive features in the Shropshire of today. The Romans moved into the Shropshire/Wales area around 52AD and set up a military camp at Wroxeter (5 miles east of Shrewsbury). This was used firstly as a base to attack the Welsh, from 58AD when Emperor Nero set out to destroy the Welsh, until 80AD, when Wroxeter was secured as a Roman stronghold, a fortress. At the end of concerted Roman military activity, the fortress became a city and at its peak from 100-200AD it was a thriving centre populated by army veterans, traders and their families. At one time this walled, fortified city that the Romans called Viriconium, covered 200 acres and with a population of 5000 it was the fourth-largest Roman settlement in Britain.

Excavations which still continue have revealed many fascinating Roman features: plaster ceilings, mosaic floors, doors with locks and padlocks, pens, tools, a forum, bath house and a water system supplied by an aqueduct almost a mile long. There are other features scattered around the county revealing the presence of the Romans but when they left, tribal elements ruled for a time and Wroxeter was at the centre of the struggle for power.

Shortly after the Romans left, tribes from what is now Germany arrived and became the dominant power between 410AD and the arrival of the Normans in 1066. A number of Shropshire village names still bear the derivation from the Anglo-Saxon, including Woolstaston, Whittington, Melverley and many more. Many Saxon buildings, particularly churches, have survived.

During their time of dominance there were four main Anglo Saxon tribal regions in Great Britain, each with its own kingdom. The Mercian Kingdom encompassed what became Shropshire and was bounded by the massive River Severn. The most prominent of the Saxon Kings during the 8th century was King Offa of Mercia. Perhaps influenced by the amazing feat of Hadrian's Roman wall,

Excavated remains of the Roman fortress at Wroxeter (or Viriconium), estimated to be the fourth-largest Roman settlement in Britain.

King Offa started a similar project, although historians believe that Offa's Dyke was more intended to serve as a demarcation line: a boundary between Mercia and the Welsh Border.

Offa's Dyke comprised a ditch on the Welsh side and a bank on the Mercian side, running for almost 180 miles from Prestatyn to Chepstow and in places it is almost 12 feet high. Over 100 miles longer than Hadrian's wall, it is the longest surviving archaeological construction in Britain.

Some experts also now believe that the less famous Wat's Dyke, previously thought to pre-date Offa's Dyke, may have been built afterwards and they are agreed that it also served as a boundary. It runs for 40 miles from Flintshire and finishes 9 miles into Shropshire, at Maesbury, by the River Severn. In places it is very close to Offa's boundary. The lack of evidence of fortifications anywhere along either construction makes it hard to believe that they were used for military purposes.

Around 800AD, new and powerful visitors with their distinctive longships sailed up the River Severn from the open sea and created a settlement by the river at Quatford, south of Bridgnorth. They were the Vikings and would be a daunting presence in Shropshire for the next two hundred years. A sea-borne warrior race, for a time they terrorised parts of Europe with their fast ships and mobile hit-and-run raids. However, they settled in England and conquered three of the Saxon Kingdoms until they were defeated at the Battle of Edington in 878 by Alfred the Great's forces, resulting in a 885 treaty dividing England into a defined Anglo-Saxon region and Viking Danelaw territory.

It was Alfred who was responsible for creating a series of fortifications at Shrewsbury and Bridgnorth, recognising the importance of controlling the River Severn; later invaders would endorse and strengthen his structures.

In 895 the Danes brought an army into Shropshire but eventually withdrew. Peace was finally secured in 1016 when a Dane,

Canute, became King of England. For a while the Shropshire area could prosper under its great farmers, tradesmen and craftsmen. The final insurgency came in 1066 when William the Conqueror triumphed at Hastings and England once again came under a powerful dominating force who would leave marks on the Shropshire landscape that remain visible a thousand years later!

Norman Barons replaced the ruling class, a new language was introduced, old strongholds were torn down and replaced by superbly crafted Norman castles and forts. Shropshire was, unusually, placed under the rule of Saxon Earl Edwin of Mercia as a reward for not resisting the Normans. However, rebellion was frequently in the air and when the Welsh attacked Shrewsbury with support from an army from Chester, William was forced to counter-attack the rebels and destroyed them.

Two years later Edwin of Mercia was murdered by his own men and William, losing patience with the Saxons, placed his long-time friend Roger de Montgomery in control of Shropshire, the region that William regarded as not only difficult but vital in settling England. He knew that control of Shropshire would prevent the Welsh from crossing the border and stirring unrest. King William replaced the Saxon timber fortifications with a string of Norman castles, forming an impressive buffer against Welsh incursions. These included Ludlow, Knighton, Bridgnorth and Shrewsbury castles. The Normans can also be regarded as the founders of Oswestry, developing the site from a small settlement and endowing it with a stone castle.

Ambitious Normans flocked to the Marches area where fame, riches and land could be earned from military service. Even today there are still Norman place names and surnames surviving in old Shropshire families.

Churches, monasteries and abbeys were constructed and one of the finest, Shrewsbury Abbey, was built by the Norman administrator Roger de Montgomery: an extremely impressive building and a sacred site for pilgrims. The Normans also augmented the cultivation of crops and cleared forested areas for grazing, encouraging communal farming while also setting aside woodlands for hunting.

The unrest along the Marcher Lands continued for several centuries and it is estimated that more than 150 castles or castle-like structures were built in Shropshire, making it the most heavily-fortified county in England. But still the Marches were a lawless area and successive English Kings, John, Henry III and Edward I all spent money and time to ensure that the Welsh were kept on their side of the border.

In 1282, in a sword fight just outside Builth, Shropshire knight Stephen Frankton killed the Welsh leader Llewelyn ap Gruffydd, but the English-Welsh struggle would continue for many years.

A Welsh rebellion led by Owain Glendower, supported by Percy the Earl of Northumberland and his son Hotspur, was heavily defeated by Henry IV's forces at the Battle of Shrewsbury on 22 July 1403. It was to be the last Welsh uprising, but soon Shropshire was caught up in the War of the Roses and Ludlow Castle was taken and sacked by the Lancastrians in 1459.

It was not until the 16th century that relative peace was brought to the lawless Welsh Border when the Council in the Marches and Wales was established and the Acts of Union ended the dominance and power of the Marcher Lords.

For more than 100 years, the fortified town of Ludlow dominated Wales. The border was re-defined and authority and responsibility vested in reliable bodies. The magnificent castles dotted around the landscape were, to all intents and purposes, defunct but now survived as centrepieces for pageants and ceremonial occasions.

Shropshire had a very high-profile visitor seeking sanctuary in September 1651. King Charles II had been defeated at the Battle of Worcester by Cromwell in the Third Civil War and fled into Shropshire, pursued by Cromwell's troops. He is said to have spent the first night at the White Ladies Priory, home of the Gifford family, just inside the Shropshire border, before trying to cross the River Severn in the Gorge. Unsuccessful, he spent the next night at Upper House, Madeley, in the barn of Francis Wolfe, the master of Coalbrookdale ironworks. The next morning the river crossing was still guarded by Cromwell's men so he went to Boscobel House, the main seat of the Gifford family, where he was forced to seek sanctuary in an oak tree on the family estate. The following day he tried again to escape and was this time successful, eventually reaching France. The story of the Boscobel Oak is now part of the folklore of Great Britain.

The Romans, the Germans, the Danes and the French have all in some way left their own distinctive marks on Shropshire.

Farming continued apace with the enclosure of open spaces and a shift from arable to pastoral with a rapid development in animal farming. Cattle, pigs and thriving sheep farming created a huge Shropshire wool industry exporting to France and to the Netherlands.

South Shropshire's natural resources, particularly of lead, had been well known to the Romans but over the centuries mining became more sophisticated and by the 1870s Shropshire was producing 10 per cent of the UK's lead output, until the industry went into sharp decline 30 years later. Coal had been mined on a small scale from the mid-16th century and was used for iron ore smelting. Later, this precious resource would provide the springboard for an era of prosperity that could only be dreamed of. The use of this fossil fuel eventually spawned a massive industry and the eyes of the world fixed on Shropshire. Industrialists, scientists, workers and visitors poured into the county in an orgy of economic boom.

In 1709 in Ironbridge, Ironmaster Abraham Darby discovered that using coke instead of charcoal for smelting reduced the impurities that spoiled the process. Coke provided a cleaner and cheaper method.

Very soon furnaces and foundries began to spring up close to iron and coal sources and close to the River Severn in such areas as Coalbrookdale. Darby established his works there and soon the whole area was a hive of activity as iron smelting went into full production. It was the start of the Industrial Revolution that would project Britain into the forefront of world trade.

Workshops and huge complexes were established for the production of iron wheels, rails, and cylinders for steam engines. This enabled Richard Trevithick to build the world's first steam locomotive. A whole range of iron products flooded out of the region and people came from all over the world to witness the 'revolution'. It was boom time and the region prospered.

It was, however, Darby's grandson Abraham Darby III who put Shropshire on the map for centuries to come, when he built the world's first cast-iron bridge in 1779. The Iron Bridge, still in use today, spans the River Severn at Ironbridge Gorge close to Coalbrookdale, and with its distinctive arch is instantly recognisable the world over.

For a time the industry was self-perpetuating: iron, coal and bitumen were local resources, the river and adjoining canals were used for transport, workers eager to join in the prosperity flooded into the coalfields and foundries and the town of Ironbridge grew by the side of the river.

The workforce had to be fed and housed, so farming and construction received a boost and a whole range of by-products evolved from the concentration of businesses: tar and varnish, dyes, tiles, bricks, glass, soap and, at Coalport, high quality world-famous porcelain was produced.

At this time, the major problem was transport, roads were generally poor and the best form of transport was river barge using the canal system and of course the Severn. Barges laden with coal, lead, wool, cheese and raw materials to supply the multifarious businesses traversed the canal system, later the Shropshire Union Canal.

The world's first cast-iron bridge, built over the River Severn near Coalbrookdale in 1779 by Abraham Darby III.

Roads started to improve during the 18th century. London could be reached from Shropshire by stagecoach in 1753 in three and a half days, but by 1772 the journey had been reduced to one and a half days. Real improvement in the road system started from around 1810 but the major new form of transport, the railway, came to Shropshire in 1837. In the early days, coaches would transfer passengers to connect to trains destined for London and Birmingham, until Shropshire had its first main railway line in 1849 and more lines were added later. By the 20th century Shrewsbury had become one of the major railway junctions in the UK.

Without question, the railways opened up Shropshire and gave it access to a whole variety of markets. Visitors, traders and businessmen were able to move about the country quickly and transport their goods to new markets. Towns like Oswestry and Shrewsbury grew quickly as a result and were able to attract customers to their specialist fields. Most market towns would have a whole variety of regular tradesmen, including drapers, cobblers, shoemakers, ironmongers, carpenters, builders and tailors but some of the towns were renowned for a particular skill. Whitchurch was renowned for clockmaking; Ludlow for gloves; Bridgnorth carpets; Oswestry, linen and bedding; but the bedrock for most of the market towns was farming.

The boom time resulted in a need for urban housing and, although most towns were lit by gas, overcrowding with workers and families crammed into tiny dwellings without adequate sanitation, sewerage or running water was in direct contrast to the houses of the wealthy merchants and businessmen, who lived away from the squalor of the inner townships, on the outskirts.

An amazing property was built in the village of Bucknell by Sir Henry Ripley MP: it had 12 chimneys, 365 windows, 7 exterior doors and 52 rooms. It was lit by electricity, had luxurious fittings and a plumbing system based on a series of hoses. Bedstone Court was completed in 1884 and the original building with it unique features and superb gallery of coloured stained-glass windows representing the four seasons, now forms the basis of a much-expanded private school, Bedstone College. Headmaster Michael Symonds and his team have established this co-educational school as one of the leaders in the county, set in superb grounds. It is another example of Shropshire using its rich heritage to ensure a bright future for today's young people.

Farming continued to sustain the county: the sheep, pigs and cattle industry was thriving and the Irish and particularly the Welsh flooded Shropshire to work in the fields with crops and the animals.

However by the early 1900s the glory days of the Industrial Revolution were waning and the iron industry went into decline.

Very soon the once-thriving metropolis around Ironbridge and Bridgnorth became a desolate oasis. Rusting furnaces, rotting work sheds, weed-smothered machinery exposed to the elements and dilapidated buildings gave little indication of what was once a vibrant, noisy centre of energy and excellence.

During the First World War, some new visitors graced Shropshire. American and Canadian soldiers fighting alongside the Allies arrived, and German prisoners were incarcerated for the duration, while the Shropshire Yeomanry and the King's Shropshire Light Infantry were fighting with distinction for their country in France. The horrors of the conflict were recorded in the distinctive poetry of Salopian Wilfred Owen who came to be regarded as the greatest of the war poets.

The promise of a 'country fit for heroes' at the war end did not materialise and the General Strike of 1926 affected the whole country. Although the decline of the iron industry was a grievous blow to Shropshire, the coal industry, although much reduced, was still in existence and Ifton Colliery, the largest in the county, still employed 1,357 men. Its closure in 1968 was virtually the end of coal mining as an industry in Shropshire.

During the Second World War in 1939, the people of Shropshire supported the war effort by working on the land to help feed the country and looking after evacuees seeking sanctuary from heavily-bombed parts of the country.

Mention must be made of the Salopians who achieved the ultimate accolade of the Victoria Cross in fighting for their country. The medal is the highest honour available to serving soldiers and is given for valour or bravery above and beyond the call of duty. On more than ten occasions, Salopians have achieved this award, among them Captain Henry Warburton-Lee (Royal Navy) from Whitchurch who was killed leading his destroyer flotilla into battle in Norway 1940, but not before sinking several enemy destroyers; and Captain John Brunt from Priestweston, who was awarded the Military Cross before being awarded the VC posthumously. After successfully defending his men and position, killing many of the attacking Italians at Faenza, he was killed by a wayward mortar shell whilst relaxing with a drink.

During the Second World War the county's warship *HMS Shropshire* was given by Winston Churchill to the Australian Navy and took part in the last great surface engagement at the Battle of Surigao Strait where she engaged the Japanese battleship *Yamashiro* and had the honour of being present when the Japanese surrendered in Tokyo Bay in September 1945.

Over the centuries the county has had several ships in the Royal Navy named after its towns. The *Shrewsbury*, launched in 1695, was broken up in 1749, to be replaced by another *Shrewsbury* in 1758 that was condemned in 1783 and then scuttled off Jamaica. The corvette *Shrewsbury Castle* was loaned to the Royal Norwegian Navy but was sunk by a mine in 1944. There have been several vessels named after Ludlow; the first in 1698 was captured by the French in 1703; the *Ludlow Castle* built in 1707 was hulked in 1743 in Antigua; another *Ludlow Castle* built in 1744 was broken up in 1771; the *Ludlow Paddle* minesweeper was sunk by a mine in 1916; and the destroyer *HMS Ludlow* was eventually beached and used as a target ship in 1945.

After the Second World War, Shropshire was for a time in the doldrums, its lead industry long since gone, the iron industry revolution a distant memory and its once-thriving coal industry all but gone by the 1960s. It had to re-invent itself. It still had a much-respected farming industry but there was a need to regenerate, and innovation was required.

Money was invested in new agricultural plant and machinery, and farms were rejuvenated, rebuilt and, with electricity and piped water helping to boost production, the farming industry was stimulated. When the largely-agricultural West Midlands Show was launched modestly in 1946, it attracted an attendance of over 30,000. Housing programmes were soon underway and in 1951 a landmark scheme saw the redevelopment of Lilleshall Hall, which became one of the UK's first residential sports centres.

The original estate and impressive mansion had been built in

1831 for the Duke of Sutherland as a country retreat. It received national recognition when the England soccer team trained there prior to winning the World Cup in 1966. Today the impressive entrance proudly proclaims 'Lilleshall National Sports Centre' and the long drive through secluded grounds passes a grand, more modern building built in the traditional style, behind which is the magnificent, original mansion house and superb gardens. The complex provides sports training and facilities both in the corporate and private sectors and is open to the public for golf, soccer, archery, swimming, gymnastics, squash etc and is rightly acclaimed as a National Centre of Sports Excellence; a prime example of utilising the past for a modern initiative.

Nevertheless, much more was needed and the late 1960s saw the launch of two initiatives that helped Shropshire back on its feet. In 1968 a new town, Telford, was authorised to be built on the derelict wasteland of the Coalbrookdale coalfield, embracing several of the smaller hamlets nearby. In 1967, the Ironbridge Gorge

Rear view of the magnificent mansion house that is now Lilleshall National Sports Centre; a National Centre of Sports excellence.

Museum Trust was established to investigate ways in which the old site could be re-generated and preserved as a heritage project.

After a slow start, Telford is now the largest town in Shropshire with a population of around 140,000. It offers a totally different experience to visitors familiar with the county's ancient towns, with its ultra-modern buildings and shopping mall.

A real success story has been the preservation and conservation of the site which set Britain on its own industrial revolution. The Ironbridge Gorge Museum Trust now embraces 10 industrial museums and the area they cover has been recognised as a Unesco World Heritage Site. Built on the foundations where it all began, museums specialising in specific areas of production such as coalport china, tiles and iron works offer visitors an all-year round opportunity to study and watch such activities as the iron smelting process, candle-making, carpentry and printing, all in renovated original buildings. In 1982 one of the huge furnaces that had been exposed to the elements and was gradually rusting away, was cleaned, restored and housed in a purpose-built building.

At Ironbridge there is also a Tar Tunnel, which visitors don safety-wear to enter and experience the distinctive smell of liquid bitumen. The whole Ironbridge conurbation is dominated by the still hugely-impressive world's first iron bridge.

Modern industry also came into the county. GKN Sankey of the motor industry was for a time the largest employer in the county. Later, the completion of the Ironbridge Power Station expansion in the late 1960s became the tallest structure in Shropshire, with a 670 foot high chimney that can be seen for miles around. Despite its size, such efforts were put into making the towers blend into their surroundings that the station was put forward for a conservation award.

Shropshire has skilfully re-invented itself and has wisely capitalised on its past to ensure its future. A particular success story based very much on the past, involves the stone industry.

Museum of the Gorge, just one of the ten museums founded by the Ironbridge Gorge Museum Trust after 1967.

The county still has a number of functioning stone quarries. Bayston Hill Quarry near Shrewsbury is one of the UK's four most important quarries. Many motorway surfaces, particularly in the West Midlands and Wales, are made from Precambrian gritstone, an aggregate called Graywacke, mined at Bayston Hill; the M6 toll road for example contains 75,000 tonnes of this gritstone! The Shropshire quarry annually mines and supplies more than 850,000 tons of the aggregate for the repair and dressing of the national motorways. Unsurprisingly the scale of such annual extraction has created a quarry 95 metres deep, 300 metres wide and more than a kilometre long.

In 2008, Bayston Hill Quarry earned national acclaim when it won a prestigious contract to supply Abu Dhabi with 4,000 tons of the specialist mineral. Formula One had granted Abu Dhabi the right to host a stage of the Formula One race season but they had to meet very specific quality standards in relation to the new 5.6

kilometre race-track being constructed in time for their first race in November 2009. Previous Bayston Hill Quarry clients in Bahrain were delighted with the quality and the track grip afforded by the gritstone surface and were happy to recommend Bayston Hill to the Abu Dhabi authorities. When the race was televised in 2009, it was interesting to note that those powerful, state-of-the-art racing cars were competing on a surface from Shropshire that first saw the light of day many millions of years ago!

Shropshire today has gravitated to a more service-oriented commercial base, with a greater emphasis on attracting visitors. Tourism is thriving. Walkers and countryside lovers flock to the world of A. E. Housman's *A Shropshire Lad*: the valleys, rolling hills and quaint little villages. The Long Mynd, Clee Hills, the Wrekin and Clun Forest are just a few of the many delights afforded to hikers, bikers and riders.

The historic landmark of Offa's Dyke offers a spectacular walk right along the English-Welsh Border for almost 177 miles and the Shropshire Way is a walk through an incredible range of landscapes for almost 140 miles. The network of canals and waterways has been reclaimed and enhanced by the Shropshire Union Canal company and affords very attractive waterway holidays enabling the tourist to view spectacular countryside at a leisurely pace. Similarly the Severn Valley Railway Preservation Society started in 1967 with the objective of operating attractive railway routes for the enjoyment of enthusiasts and tourists.

Although the county has no large cities, it has 22 towns, only six of which are considered of any significant size: the county town of Shrewsbury, Telford, Oswestry, Newport, Bridgnorth and Ludlow. Shropshire is Britain's largest inland county i.e. with no part directly bordering onto the sea.

It is also one of Britain's most beautiful regions, with its valleys, rivers, tiny hamlets, fortified mansions, superb stone castles, numerous medieval buildings and ancient partial walls proudly acknowledging their rich and historic past.

It is no wonder then that Shropshire has been used as the setting for so many films, television series and books.

It is claimed that the Hollywood couple, Harrison Ford and Calista Flockhart have cruised the county's canals during a break from filming, but many other famous thespians have spent time in the county before them. Film stars Keira Knightley and James McAvoy filmed the box office hit, *Atonement* at Stokesay Court, near Ludlow; in 1978 actor Richard Burton filmed *Absolution* at Ellesmere College; John Cleese came to Much Wenlock to make the 1980 film *Clockwise*; Hugh Grant used Hampton Loade near Oswestry for *The Englishman Who Went Up A Hill But Came Down A Mountain*; the Oscar-winning film *Howards End* brought Anthony Hopkins and Emma Thompson to Brampton Bryan; and in 1984 *A Christmas Carol* was filmed in Shrewsbury where the cast and production team took over the *Prince Rupert Hotel* and after filming was over, St Chad's Church in Shrewsbury was left with a souvenir – the headstone of Ebenezer Scrooge!

Much Wenlock was also the setting for the film *Gone to Earth*, adapted from the novel by Shropshire author Mary Webb; atmospheric Hawkstone Park was the ideal setting for the BBC's *The Chronicles of Narnia*; Ludlow's Castle Lodge featured in ITV's *Moll Flanders*; the novel *Blott on the Landscape* by Tom Sharpe was about Shropshire and was filmed in Ludlow; Blists Hill featured in *Doctor Who*; Chirk Castle in *Casanova*; and *The Green, Green Grass* television series featured the Ludlow countryside.

Shropshire has been linked with some of Great Britain's most important figures: Owain Glendower, King John, Henry III, Edward I and Charles II reflect the frequently violent times in the history of the county and the nation.

One of this country's more charismatic politicians Benjamin Disraeli learnt his trade as Member of Parliament for Shrewsbury from 1841-1847. He went on to become Prime Minister of Great

Britain in 1868 and again in 1874 before being ousted by Gladstone in 1880. Charles Dickens wrote *The Pickwick Papers* at the 16th century coaching inn, the *Lion Hotel* in Shrewsbury. There, in 1833, the world-renowned violinist Paganini also stayed for a time and performed a concert.

Emperor Haile Selassie of Ethiopia visited Shropshire and is reputed to have stayed at Milebrook House, Knighton, on the Wales/Shropshire border and President Charles de Gaulle was a regular visitor when his family sought sanctuary in Britain during World War II by renting Gadlas Hall, Dudleston Heath, Ellesmere.

In 1998 Shropshire attracted world-wide attention when the beautiful 1,000 acre estate at Weston Park, Shifnal, played host to world leaders as the venue for the G8 Summit Meeting. The site has existed since the 11th century but today's manor house was built in 1671 as the ancestral home of the Earl of Bradford. The mansion houses priceless art treasures and together with its lakes, woods and landscaped gardens is held in trust for the nation. The Queen and Princess Anne have honoured the county with many visits though the latest member of the Royal family to come to Shropshire was Prince Harry, who in May 2009 was sent to RAF Shawbury to begin ground school training in his determination to qualify as a helicopter pilot.

This book records in more detail certain individuals who have represented the county on the national and international stage and who have enriched the lives of their fellow countrymen through their deeds or skills. These people were born or brought up in the county and can be considered Salopians. However, there is a group of people who were educated in Shropshire, more specifically Shrewsbury School, who have contributed greatly to our society politically and culturally and who are worthy of mention.

Old Shrewsbury School pupils include Michael Heseltine, who became a Conservative Cabinet Minister and was at one time Deputy Leader of the Conservative Party; Michael Palin, who made his name with the hugely successful Monty Python's Flying Circus and who is now somewhat of a national treasure with his round-the-world travel documentaries; the late Willie Rushton, renowned for his wit as an actor, author and gifted cartoonist as well as a broadcaster; Christopher Timothy who played that popular Yorkshire vet James Herriot in the television series *All Creatures Great and Small*; the late John Peel, iconic Radio DJ so beloved by his fans; Richard Ingrams, writer of satire and wit and editor of *Private Eye* for many years who also wrote news columns for *The Spectator* and *The Observer* and today runs his own magazine *The Oldie*.

Another old Shrewsbury boy of the *Private Eye* writers club was the late Paul Foot. Foot, who died in 2004, was renowned for his left-wing politics and was constantly campaigning in the *Daily Mirror* and *The Guardian* against miscarriages of justice, for which he was awarded the Journalist of the Year accolade on three occasions. All in their own fields of expertise each of them helped entertain and enrich the lives of their fellow citizens.

Shropshire: historically violent, geographically diverse, industrially vibrant, culturally profuse, has much to commend it and has demonstrated that it has been able to manage change and adapt to challenging times.

Chapter Two

FAMOUS SALOPIANS

Clive of India 1725-1774

We headed cross-country for mile after mile down tiny, rutted, extremely narrow country lanes determined to find the birthplace of one of England's greatest historical figures. We were on the trail of a man whose exploits in 18th century India secured the continent and paved the way for global British dominance in the later Victorian era; a man whose early years were given over to mischief, but who would later be regarded as a genius. It is a fact that many of the great figures of world history were flawed individuals and psychologists believe that there is a small dividing line between madness and genius. Sometimes that madness ignores all logic and reason and a subsequent achievement against all the odds is the result.

Eventually our patience and persistence were rewarded when near to the tiny village of Moreton Say we came upon Styche Hall, the birthplace of Robert Clive, or Clive of India as he would later be called, born here in September 1725. Styche Hall had once been a gracious residence but is now divided into apartments – though it is a great pity that it could not have been preserved for the nation as an historic museum.

Clive's father had an unspectacular career as a lawyer but he and his wife had thirteen children, of whom eight survived. The Clives fell upon difficult times and their eldest son Robert was sent, at the age of three, to live with relatives near Manchester. It is believed that they delighted in him and spoilt him, though noting his quick temper, and by the time he returned to his parents in Shropshire the die was cast: he was used to getting his own way. When he was aged seven or eight, he attended the Old Grammar School in Market Drayton, but was not renowned for his academic ability.

Rebellious and ill-disciplined, his early escapades were more boyish feats of physical daring, such as the time he climbed the tower of St Mary's Church in Market Drayton and shouted at the passers-by, while clinging precariously to a gargoyle. Further

Styche Hall in Moreton Say, birthplace of Lord Robert Clive of India.

misdemeaners included a group of boys insulting and 'shop-lifting' from local tradesmen, which greatly infuriated his lawyer father.

His parents dispatched him to work for the East India Company in Madras as a clerk at about the age of 18, in the hope that he would create some much-needed wealth for his family, comprising largely of sisters! The long sea voyage to India, disease, and the harsh living conditions meant that many did not complete the journey, but Clive survived.

Far from home and operating in a disciplined environment, he became bored and homesick. It was perhaps at this time that Clive's illness, diagnosed many years later as manic depression, manifested itself for the first time. At one stage the only way out of his dilemma, he believed, was suicide and it is reputed that he pointed a gun at his temple and pulled the trigger. Silence. He primed the pistol, tried again, and once again had no result. He took this as a sign that perhaps he was destined for greater things: how prophetic.

Destiny was to beckon him at the age of 21, when hostilities between the British and the French for the control of India started in earnest. In 1746 the French captured Madras where Clive was working, but he and a handful of others managed to escape to the British positions at Fort George. The excitement, danger, and sense of adventure appealed to everything in Robert Clive and he joined the East India Company's private army and for the first time found his niche in life.

Very soon, his reputation for courage and daring began to get him noticed. His first action of note was when he commanded a force of 200 Europeans and 300 Indian troops and, with only a handful of guns, seized the fort at Argot. Despite being attacked by a superior force of French and Indian troops, he held out for more than 50 days. The enemy, in a last desperate assault led by armoured elephants, were beaten off and Clive was on his way into the history books.

His reputation in India and England soared and Prime Minister William Pitt declared the 27-year-old Robert Clive to be a 'heaven-born general'. In the meantime, he was also enjoying the social rounds in India and had met a young English girl, Margaret Maskelyne, the sister of a close friend. She was small, pretty and intelligent and for a time they courted although Clive, it is reported, was in the meantime able to satisfy his needs in the bars and brothels of Madras. Nevertheless, the couple married on 18 February 1753 and set sail home for England the following day on the seven-month voyage. He went on to be a devoted husband, as evidenced by his letters, and a long-term and loyal friend to all his companions.

So Clive returned to England a wealthy married man; Margaret gave birth to two children and they settled in some style into a fine London house. However, he hadn't forgotten Shropshire and he paid for the re-building of the old family home at Styche Hall as well as buying Walcot Hall and its Estate at Lydbury North in 1763.

After only three years of basking in his wealth and reputation, Clive hankered for action and returned to India with Margaret. He was first appointed Lieutenant Colonel and then Deputy Governor of Madras, quite a change from his early days in that city as a junior clerk.

The war in India had returned with a vengeance and the Indians, under the Nawab of Bengal, Siraj ud Daula, had captured Calcutta from the British. However, the world was shocked and horrified when news came that on 20 June 1756, 146 British prisoners had been locked overnight in a tiny room in stifling heat and when the door was opened the following morning 123 had died! The notorious event was remembered as The Black Hole of Calcutta and would ensure that any British retaliation would be ruthless. Meanwhile, back in England, one of the Clive's sons had died and then in Calcutta their third child, a daughter, died. It was a terrible time for Margaret, as she had to bear the brunt of the sorrow while her husband was engaged in the war. They were in love and she called him in one of her letters, 'the comfort of my life'.

Colonel Robert Clive assembled his forces, quickly retook Calcutta and then met Siraj ud Daula and his vastly superior forces at Plassey on 23 June 1757, the battle that would secure Clive's place in history and begin the British dominance in India that would last for the next two hundred years. Genius or madness? Clive's forces of 800 European troops and 2,100 Indian infantry supported by eight field guns were set against 35,000 Indian infantry and 15,000 cavalry supported by 53 guns. Yet a combination of good luck and Clive's shrewdness ensured a resounding British victory at Plassey.

The aftermath was, from Clive's benefit, very financially rewarding. The new Nawab, following the assassination of Siraj ud Daula, gave Clive a sum of around £234,000 as a form of indemnity – an enormous fortune in those days.

After a job well done, Clive settled in Bengal, but in 1760, after persuasion from Margaret, returned to England. She was pregnant again but sadly just before sailing lost the baby.

Once back in England, life was good for a time. They were reunited with their son Ned and Margaret went on to give birth to three daughters. In that same year, at the age of 34, Clive was elected MP for Shrewsbury and also became Mayor of the town. He was a local, national and international figure.

In his absence from India, his good order had been replaced by corruption and although Clive was not in the best of health in 1765, he once again returned there to restore order. Margaret had insisted that he should go and was adamant that she would accompany him. She explained her loyalty and determination thus: 'to follow the fortune of my first and best friend, my husband'.

But fate intervened once again and Margaret was unable to leave with him when she discovered that she was pregnant. Clive was upset at losing her company and declared, 'God only knows how much I have suffered in my separation from the best of my women.'

Steady on Clive. That statement seems to raise a lot of questions!

The journeys to India were daunting even for someone in robust health. Clive was increasingly dependent on opium to control acute abdominal pain.

Unsurprisingly there was resentment in India when Clive started to investigate corruption practices and soon fingers were pointed at him, as clearly he had become a wealthy man following his exploits in India. It wasn't a triumphant time for him with all the backbiting and controversy and he missed Margaret and the children terribly.

He was relieved to return to England in 1767 but had to face a certain amount of acrimony and questions as to his own honesty and ethics in accepting huge sums of money from grateful Indian leaders. Although it brought him under the microscope, it was still acknowledged in India that he had rendered great service to Britain. His main problem was that he didn't belong to the Establishment – he was very rich, but he was from the provincial middle classes at a time when it was important to be in the landed, aristocratic set. Clive was bound to suffer from scurrilous stories.

Nevertheless, his popularity among the British populace was undamaged and in 1774 he resumed the role of MP for Shrewsbury with an increased majority.

Tragedy continually stalked the family when their fourth daughter died, leaving them with one son, Ned, and three daughters from Margaret's eight or so pregnancies. The routines of domestic life and the absence of action did not suit Clive's flamboyant personality. At the age of 49, on 22 November 1774, Clive of India was found dead at his house in Berkeley Square, London. He had taken his own life. Initially there was some attempt to gloss over the question of suicide because to take one's own life in those days was a sin, and unacceptable behaviour in a national hero. However, reliable evidence has it that he cut his throat and that it was Margaret who discovered his body in a pool of blood. Shocked and traumatised, she suffered memory-loss over the death and family and friends were able to assure her that he had died of a stroke. Clive had suffered greatly: his history of manic depression, his abdominal pain and reliance on opium, perhaps the criticism levelled at him despite his exploits in serving his country had fuelled his depression and led to his ending what had become a miserable life.

His body was returned to Moreton Say and buried inside St Margaret's church. There is a plaque on the wall inside the church with the inscription:

Sacred to the Memory of Robert Lord Clive KB, Buried within the walls of this church.

Born Sept 29 1725
Died Nov 22 1774
Primus in Indis.

The local vicar kindly showed me around the church and pointed out the spot where, during church renovations, a sealed lead coffin had been discovered. To fashion a coffin from lead was an expensive process, which indicated that the body must have been that of someone very important. Clive was the most likely candidate. At the time of writing, permission to open the coffin to verify the incumbent had been refused.

Undefeated in battle, with victories against overwhelming odds at Calcutta, Plassey, Trichinopoly and several skirmishes in Bengal, a true giant of British history was defeated by life itself.

Clive of India's legacy lives on in Shropshire today, though. After his second tour of India, Robert Clive stayed at Pézenas in the south of France. While there, he gave them the recipe for a bite-sized mutton and chutney pie (a petit paté) which they still enjoy there today, consuming over 200,000 each year. They also produce a Lord Clive wine in the local vineyards. This relationship between Pézenas and Market Drayton has resulted in the thriving twinning of the two towns today.

Left:
Statue of Lord Robert
Clive, Clive of India,
located on The Square in
the heart of Shrewsbury.

Right:
The Clive family tomb in the
grounds of St Margaret's church
in Moreton Say.

41

Charles Robert Darwin 1809-1882

If one Shropshire giant helped shape the world, another shook the world and for a time created a controversy that raged between scholars and the church, when Charles Darwin propounded his theory in 1859 on the origin of species and suggested natural selection and the survival of the fittest was a prerequisite in the evolutionary process.

Interestingly, as the world celebrated the 200th anniversary of Darwin's birth in 2009, an egg collected by him on his historic voyage on *HMS Beagle,* which started in 1831, was discovered by a volunteer in the Zoology Museum of Cambridge University. The cracked egg was one of 16 bird eggs collected between 1831 and 1836 and belonged to the Tinamou bird of Uruguay. Its presence was unknown until the volunteer found a little box with C. Darwin written on it and surmised that Darwin himself had cracked the egg by packing it into too tiny a box.

Charles Robert Darwin was born on 12 February 1809 at Mount House in the Frankwell area of Shrewsbury, the fifth child of six born to father Robert, a wealthy society doctor and financier, and wife Susanna. Charles' paternal grandfather, Erasmus Darwin, was a prominent physician, scientist and poet. On his mother's side Charles' grandfather was Josiah Wedgwood, whose name lives on worldwide over two hundred years after his death, defined by the manufacture of his distinctive pottery.

The young Darwin grew up in Shrewsbury, and the Shrewsbury School of his day is now the town library. He attended the school with older brother Erasmus and they became boarders when their mother died in 1817. Today outside Shrewsbury library is a statue of its most famous former pupil.

It was around the age of eight that Darwin started to take an interest in nature but his father was steering him towards a career in medicine. In 1825 he spent most of the summer acting as an assistant to his father in the treatment of the poor of the county. Later that year, at the age of 16, he went to Edinburgh University to study medicine but quickly came to the conclusion that a medical career was not for him. He found it boring and gruesome and started to neglect his medical studies in favour of natural history. In somewhat of a quandary, in 1827 his father enrolled him at Christ's College, Cambridge, with the intention of directing him into life as a clergyman.

Darwin rebelled. He was more interested in riding, shooting, and studying marine invertebrates and plants. He started collecting beetles and joined the natural history group. His interests brought him under the influence of the leading naturalists in Cambridge and in particular botanist and geologist John Stevens Henslow. He was also fascinated by natural theology.

The summer of 1831 was spent on an expedition in Wales and on his return he discovered that Henslow had recommended him to go as a naturalist on a self-funded two-year expedition on the ship, *HMS Beagle*, captained by Robert Fitzroy. Darwin hardly dared mention it to his father and when he did, the answer was a resounding 'no'. The world can thank Josiah Wedgwood who eventually persuaded his brother-in-law to let the young Charles Darwin go on what would prove to be the journey of a lifetime. They set sail on 27 December 1831 as part of the Royal Navy surveying expedition visiting Cape Verde, other Atlantic islands, South America, the Galapagos Islands, Tahiti, New Zealand, Australia, Tasmania, Keeling Island, the Maldives, Mauritius, St Helena, Ascension Island and Brazil. The odyssey lasted five years.

Ostensibly, Darwin was there as a naturalist and he took advantage of the fantastic opportunity offered to him. He noted, listed, examined and categorised birds, plant and animal species and their differences and similarities from place to place. In particular he observed animals that had been confined to islands and noted their development and differences from those of the same species on the mainland. He also made comparisons between present species and fossils from those extinct.

He noted how animals evolved to suit their surroundings, in order to ensure their survival. In particular, he observed the way in which mocking birds of the same species on the South American mainland had differences to those confined on the islands. Similarly, the same breed of tortoise had slightly differing shapes from island to island. Those that could not adapt, he observed, invariably perished. It was the formation of his theory on the transmutation of species. He discovered seashells high up on cliff tops and fossils of large mammals long since extinct. His curiosity was aroused and he made copious notes of his findings.

When the voyage was over, Darwin returned to England in October 1836 to discover that he was somewhat of a celebrity, for John Henslow had circulated the geological letters he had sent him to selected naturalists.

After spending some time with his family in Shrewsbury he went to Cambridge and then to London and spent a period of intense pressure working on his journal, recording his findings, lecturing and attending meetings. In June 1837 the stress had overtaken him and he was beset by illness. Abdominal pain, palpitations, nervousness and frequent bouts of stomach sickness forced him to take a break with his Wedgwood relatives at Maer Hall, Staffordshire. He got to know his cousin Emma Wedgwood and was impressed by her charm and intelligence. However, he felt driven to finish his deliberations following the voyage, despite his frequent bouts of illness. In the midst of his daunting workload, he was elected fellow of the Royal Geographical Society and in July headed for Maer Hall and Emma.

It was 11 November before he plucked up the courage and proposed to her and she accepted. She was clearly a caring woman and ideal for him at this stage in his life, as revealed in a letter to him: 'so don't be ill any more my dear Charley till I can be with you to nurse you'.

A delighted Charles found a cottage for them in Gower Street, London and after they married at Maer Hall on 29 January 1839, they returned to London by train to start their new life.

The next few years were busy and in 1843 the family moved to Down House, in Kent, a more appropriate country location for a botanist. Charles continued to write geological and botanical books and in 1853 as a botanist he received the Royal Medal from the Royal Society for his work. Nevertheless, his poor health continued and when in 1851 their first child Annie died at the age of ten they were distraught.

Darwin continued to work on his theories of evolution and was almost at the point of publication when naturalist Alfred Russel Wallace surprised Darwin and his supporters by sending him a communication revealing that he had come to the same conclusion as Darwin on the natural selection theory. In order to satisfy honour on both sides, the men issued a joint publication although Darwin's theories went further than Wallace's. It was during this time that tragedy once again struck the Darwins. In the middle of the Wallace revelation, the village of Downe in Kent had been hit with scarlet fever and Darwin's baby son had died.

Despite this setback which devastated the family man for a time, he finished his book. *The Origin of Species*, propounding Darwin's theory on evolution and the transmutation of species through natural selection, was published in 1859 and immediately caused a public furore. The church in particular bitterly attacked his theories and Darwin and his friends were constantly called upon to justify his conclusions. Darwinism stiumulated argument, debate and controversy but today his work is accepted for what it was: a brilliant piece of scientific research and deduction that has withstood all attempts to disprove it.

In 1871 Darwin re-ignited the controversy when publishing *The Descent of Man*, which put forward the idea that mankind was descended from African apes. He suggested that his theory would be proven if and when fossil evidence of human skulls was found. He was right: such evidence has since proven beyond doubt that mankind has descended and evolved from the ape and very possibly the African ape.

The Darwins had ten children, two of whom died in infancy and young Annie, who died at the age of ten. Three of their surviving sons went on to distinguish themselves: George as an astronomer, Francis as a botanist and Horace as a civil engineer and they all became Fellows of the Royal Society.

Despite being in frail health for much of his life, Charles Darwin died at his home in Kent nursed by Emma and his children on 19 April 1882 at the age of 73.

Around the world there are geographical features commemorating this most brilliant of scientists: the capital city of Australia's Northern Territory is named Darwin after him and there is a Charles Darwin National Park and a Charles Darwin University also in Australia. Mount Darwin is in the Andes and two water channels are called Darwin Sound. There is the Charles Darwin College at Cambridge University.

In 2008 came a somewhat late apology from the Church of England to Darwin's descendants for having 'misunderstood him and misrepresented him to others'. A little late and, as science has proved, totally unnecessary because Darwin's theories were based on fact not ideology.

The year 2009 was the 200th anniversary of his birth and the 150th anniversary of the publication of *Origin of Species* and Darwin Day was celebrated worldwide with the UK issuing a commemorative £2 coin.

In a recent survey Charles Darwin was listed as the 16th most influential person in world history and in a British survey he was voted 4th in the Top 100 Briton's throughout history, one place above Shakespeare. He has been honoured with his portrait on the £10 note.

This Shropshire man has shaped international thought about Man's position in the Universe.

Statue of Charles Darwin in front of the public library in Shrewsbury, formerly the home of Shrewsbury School.

Wilfred Owen 1893-1918

A Salopian who achieved world-wide fame posthumously and would be enormously gratified to find that his work today features on many university and college curricula is the internationally-respected Great War poet Wilfred Owen, who was born in Oswestry on 18 March 1893.

The horrors of the First World War, which resulted in over 20 million casualties and 8 million deaths, gave rise to a whole new genre of literature: war poetry. A number of poets adhered to the party line and wrote stirring poems of patriotism and nationalism, glorying in fighting for the cause and country. However, as the horrific statistics from the killing fields mounted, some poets questioned the validity of the sacrifice and dared to question the politicians. They spoke for the British soldier, the 'Tommy', whose life was regarded as expendable. The works of some of the more established poets who were serving officers were published almost immediately for an eager public: Rupert Brooke, Robert Graves, Charles Sorley. Less famous, but a favourite of mine, was Sergeant Joe Lee of the Black Watch.

The poets Siegfried Sassoon and the young Wilfred Owen also elected to describe the suffering and sheer horror of trench warfare in their poetry. Sassoon was the first to voice his opinion and was regarded by the establishment as practically a traitor, certainly disastrous for morale. They suggested that he was insane and sent him to a recovery hospital. Sassoon unquestionably inspired Owen to perfect his writing and Owen adopted a similar anti-war stance. Despite their views, both men served their country with distinction and were awarded the Military Cross for bravery. Sassoon's poetry quickly received acclaim but Owen was not yet established in the genre, and his work was not to be acknowledged until well after the end of the war.

Wilfred Owen's father Tom, a railway clerk whose working class parents had moved to Shrewsbury from Nantwich in 1891, married Susan, daughter of the wealthy Salter family. At first they lived in Susan's large family house, Plas Wilmot, Oswestry and Tom had to get used to a lifestyle, including servants, so very different to his own upbringing.

Their first child, Wilfred Owen, was born at Plas Wilmot and his sister Mary was born there three years later, in 1896. The family fell into financial difficulties and were forced to sell the house and around 1897 moved into Wilmot House, Canon Street, Shrewsbury.

The Owens' third child, William Harold Owen, was born at Wilmot House and the family spent the next three years living in Shrewsbury. During this time young Wilfred went to the local infants school and judging by a letter written to his mother when he was five, he was extremely literate from a young age. Many years later, amongst the 550 letters written by Owen to his mother, this first one, written in 1898, was found in a jewellery box marked 'Wilfie's first letter, 1898'.

In February 1900, Tom Owen was appointed stationmaster in Birkenhead and the family were once again on the move.

Birkenhead was a great contrast to the rural retreat of Wilmot House and the genteel Owen family were regarded as outsiders. Wilfred was educated at the Preparatory Department of the Birkenhead Institute. He was an avid reader and did well at writing, winning second prize at the end of term.

His mother Susan was already influencing him and directing him towards the church. He enrolled at Christ Church Sunday School and it was Susan who studied the bible with him and was constantly at his side.

In 1906, Tom received another promotion and the family were back on the road to Shrewsbury. The Owens for a time moved in with Tom's parents before settling in Underdale Road,

Shrewsbury. Wilfred and Harold went to Shrewsbury Borough Technical School in the spring of 1907.

Wilfred was altogether more serious than brother Harold, preferring great literature to his father's interests in sport or the sea. Wilfred remained keen on the church and would accompany his mother Susan to St Julians at the top of the hill at Wyle Cop. She was very protective, very controlling and quick to dismiss any interest he may have had in the opposite sex.

Occasionally his father would resent their closeness and would flare into a temper through his frustration at not being able to share common interests with his eldest son. Revealingly, at the end of Wilfred Owen's life it was discovered that he had written over 550 letters to his mother but only four letters to his father!

In 1910 the Owens moved to a large rented property at Mahim, Monkmoor Road and Wilfred, now 17, was restless and beginning to think about his future. His mother was pushing him firmly towards a career in the church, but Wilfred was contemplating teaching languages.

A year later, as part of his obsession with Keats, he wrote his first poem *To Poesy*, which some scholars believe was also the first revelation of his struggle with his sexuality.

Under his mother's persuasive influence, he agreed to go as a Parish Assistant to the Vicar of Dunsden and arrived in October 1911 at the twelve bed-roomed vicarage that would not only be his home for the next ten months but would also shape his destiny.

Although he was conscientious and popular with the parishioners, the constant examining, debate and discussion of faith and belief disillusioned him. He still yearned for a life devoted to poetry, and in February 1913 it was mutually agreed with the vicar that his term of secondment be terminated. Although he remained on good terms and would visit the parish in the ensuing years, he finally decided that a life in the clergy was not for him, irrespective of his mother's wishes.

He was taken ill with pneumonia and while recuperating at home, nursed by his mother, he turned once again to writing poetry. He was also still hoping for a career in teaching, for which he needed to obtain a scholarship to University College, Reading. Despite his efforts, he failed to obtain the scholarship he needed.

During this difficult time he wrote two poems and after visiting the Shrewsbury Flower Show he was inspired to write a sonnet about roses.

Nevertheless, he was struggling with not only his sexuality but also his identity and in September 1913 he left for Bordeaux to teach English. He was at last free from his mother, free from the church and he celebrated his new-found independence by taking up smoking. However he became ill with the long hours and the stress; he was exhausted and missed his mother during that first Christmas spent alone. After just over a year he left the French school to act as a private tutor to a wealthy family at their summer villa in the Pyrenees.

Owen's sexuality was once again tested when it became apparent that the mother and daughter found him attractive. The mother in particular did not appreciate him rejecting her. While working for this family he was introduced to the French poet Laurent Tailhade who was an influential mover of the Decadent set. Laurent was bisexual and appeared to be attracted to Owen, although there is no evidence of any relationship. After his seven-week appointment he returned to Bordeaux to find the school now closed and was forced to seek freelance work and find lodgings elsewhere with friends.

Wilfred had done well in Bordeaux away from his mother's influence, though she was constantly in touch. He was his own boss and enjoyed life. Author and poet Robert Graves revealed years later that Owen had hinted to him of homosexual liaisons in the clubs and bars of Bordeaux although there is and has been no conclusive evidence of that. But the call to arms was being heard throughout England and France and many of his contemporaries were joining up, including the elderly Tailhade.

Wilfred returned to London on 12 September 1915 and went to the Artists and Rifles HQ in London to undertake a medical in order to enlist. He began his training with the Artists and Rifles in London in October 1915. In contrast to his army activities, he visited the poetry bookshop owned by writer Harold Monro, the founder of *Poetry Review*, and bought several books including A. E. Housman's, *A Shropshire Lad*.

After intensive training in bayonet combat, shooting, digging trenches and erecting defensive positions in Romford, Owen returned to London where Monro viewed Owen's poetry to date, non-war of course and was very impressed.

In May 1916 he went home to Shrewsbury on leave to find that his brother Harold was away in the navy, his youngest brother Colin was working on the farm and his sister Mary was nursing. In June, Wilfred was appointed 2nd Lieutenant in the Artists and Rifles and was then transferred to the Manchester Regiment. However he wrote to his mother in August saying that he wished that he was able to join the Royal Flying Corps: 'I will yet swoop over Wrekin with the strength of a thousand eagles and all you shall see me light upon the racecourse.'

After more training, some of it at Oswestry, Owen was finally posted to France on 29 December 1916.

His first action was at Beaumont Hamel in January 1917 and he acquitted himself well, but was for the first time exposed to the horrors that would become the norm. He fell into a cellar and was for 24 hours badly concussed and badly affected by a shell exploding near him that blew apart the already-dead body of a fellow officer. Several of his friends were killed in this engagement.

The concussion was more severe than at first realised and it was later thought that Owen was suffering from delayed neurasthenia. Whatever the diagnosis, he was confused, depressed and distant, his commanding officer at the time taking this for cowardice.

Owen was sent to a hospital in Netley, Wales, to recuperate and from there to Craiglockhart Hospital, Edinburgh with the instruction that he was to see no active service for six months. It was here in August 1917 that he met Sassoon, who had been sent as a result of some of his anti-war writings to 'convalesce' (as the politicians called it.) The two men exchanged views on poetry, Sassoon was very much the mentor. It is true to say that in those first few weeks Sassoon was unimpressed with Owen's work but he began to influence the style of the impressionable young would-be poet.

On 30 October 1917 Owen was discharged as fit for duty and immediately set off for Shrewsbury where he was re-united with his delighted mother but rather cooler father. He was sent to Scarborough for training where he wrote poetry in-between sessions and sent some of his work to Robert Graves who, although much impressed, urged both Owen and Sassoon to lift their dark mood. After a further spell of training at Ripon, Owen went home on 9 April for what turned out to be his last leave with his family, and fortunately met up again with brother Harold who was also on leave.

On June 1918 Wilfred Owen was passed fit by the Medical Board in Scarborough. Shortly afterwards he heard that Sassoon had been wounded in action, which made him all the more determined to get back into action and be the voice of the ordinary fighting British 'Tommy'.

However, his immediate plans were thwarted when he failed a follow-up medical due to a heart defect. His mother and several of his close friends were secretly delighted that this failure meant the end of Owen's war. When he met Sassoon in London for lunch, Sassoon also expressed his relief that Owen would no longer be called upon to fight. Nevertheless, Owen was now in a fragile mental state and he wanted to fight to fulfil his vision and also eradicate the negative suggestions of 'cowardice' arising from his previous illness. He wrote a very emotional letter to his mother in which he poured out his feelings.

He went once again for another medical and this time was passed fit and went home to Shrewsbury to put his affairs in order. He collected all his works and entrusted them to his mother in case he did not return. Along with his mother and brother Colin they spent a last day together at Hastings and after a day in London he left for the Western Front. He was assigned to the Manchester Regiment and was at Amiens in September 1918. It was widely believed that at last, the war was about to end: the Germans had launched a massive offensive earlier in 1918 which had been blunted by the Allies, who were now pushing the Germans back on all fronts.

Around October 1918 Owen sent three poems to Sassoon and in several letters to his mother he was upbeat and jovial. He was proving to be a good officer and was well-respected by the men under his command. At the beginning of that month, when his Company Commander had been wounded, Owen had taken command and, when a German counter-attack threatened their position, Owen dashed across the open ground to an exposed position in full view of the British and Germans and, operating a captured machine gun, he personally held the sector, killing a number of the enemy. He was awarded the Military Cross for his outstanding bravery. He did not live to receive it.

On 4 November 1918, as Owen was crossing the Sambre-Oise canal by raft with his men, he was hit by German machine-gun fire and killed. Just one week later the war was over. On 5 November the *London Gazette* carried the belated news that 2nd Lieutenant Wilfred Owen had been promoted to full Lieutenant. The news that he had been awarded the Military Cross, one of the highest decorations available in the British Army, was announced on 8 November. It was only as the Shrewsbury Abbey bells were ringing out to celebrate the armistice, on 11 November 1918, that the telegram informing his parents of Wilfred's death was delivered to them at their home in Monkton Road.

His mother and father were much comforted when two of Owen's former colleagues came to visit them to pay their respects, but also to tell them that their son had been much liked and had died a brave officer.

It is often the case with a genius that they are not appreciated in their lifetime, and that is certainly true of Wilfred Owen. He had only five poems published during his lifetime but his reputation has soared in the ensuing years.

Shortly after his death, his mother arranged with Osbert Sitwell to have seven of his poems published in a 1919 anthology, but it was Siegfried Sassoon who became executor of the 100 or so works he had written. *Wilfred Owen: Poems* was published by Chatto and Windus in 1920. In 1931 Edmund Blunden wrote a rather sanitised biography of him, which had been somewhat censored by the Owen family.

Memorial to Wilfred Owen in the grounds of Shrewsbury Abbey. The inscribed words are from Owen's poem 'Strange Meeting': 'I am the enemy you killed, my friend.'

Since then there have been several versions of Owen's life published and he is generally regarded today as the greatest of all the First World War Poets.

There are memorials to Wilfred Owen in Oswestry, Shrewsbury, Birkenhead, Manchester Cathedral, and Gailly, France.

Although there is a memorial to him in the grounds of Shrewsbury Abbey, he is buried in France where he fell.

Charles Darwin, Clive of India and Wilfred Owen MC are figures of international renown. However, there are a number of Salopians whose contribution at national level is worthy of acknowledgement.

Mary Webb 1881-1927

Plagued by ill-health for much of her young life, Mary Webb was born in the small village of Leighton, near Shrewsbury, in 1881 and through her many romantic novels and poetry, she contributed greatly to the literary history of this country.

From her schoolteacher father, she inherited her love of literature and of the Shropshire countryside. On her mother's side she had the influence of the descendants of Sir Walter Scott.

When Mary was just out of her teens, she was diagnosed with a thyroid disorder that was to affect the rest of her short life. In 1912 she married Henry Webb, a teacher who was very supportive of her writing. They moved to Weston-super-Mare but soon returned to her native Shropshire where she indulged her love of nature by briefly running a market garden with her husband before he returned to his profession as a teacher.

From 1914 to 1916 they lived near the village of Pontesbury in the aptly named Rose Cottage and it was here that she wrote her first novel *The Golden Arrow*. In 1957, the village commemorated her association when the Mary Webb School and Science College was opened.

Buoyed by her first literary success, the Webbs bought land at Lyth Hill, Bayston Hill and built Spring Cottage there. She continued to write and her novels were invariably set in Shropshire, her characters allegedly based on local people she had met. *Gone to Earth*, published in 1917, is a romantic tragedy based around a simple but beautiful country girl who has a pet fox. Caught up in a romantic triangle, the heroine comes to a tragic end.

Another novel, *The House in Dormer Forest*, was published in 1920 and, when Henry Webb wanted to take up the offer of a teaching job in London, they believed the move would also enhance Mary's profile and ensure greater success. They bought a home in London, returning to Spring Cottage at weekends and school holidays.

Mary did benefit from London, meeting other writers and editors and for a time was a reviewer for *The Spectator* and *The Bookman*. But great success as a writer escaped her.

In 1922, *Seven for a Secret* was published and, two years later, there followed her most famous work *Precious Bane*. It tells the story of a young girl who, around 1816, was deemed by her neighbours to be a witch because of her prominent hare lip, and who later falls in love with a visiting weaver.

But literary recognition and financial benefits still failed to materialise. Frustration at this and her increasingly poor health contributed to the breakdown of her marriage and she returned alone to Spring Cottage in 1927. Months later, she passed away aged just 46 at St Leonard's on Sea. Mary Webb is buried in Shrewsbury's main cemetery at Longdon Road.

Although she had received the Prix Femina Vie Heureuse for *Precious Bane*, it was the only real recognition that she received during her lifetime for her published works.

Her first champion of note had been the Prime Minister Stanley Baldwin, who at a Literary Fund dinner just after her death, hailed her work and insisted that she was an unrecognised genius.

His comments galvanised the literary world, and the publisher Jonathan Cape reprinted her collected works in a standard edition. This book became a best-seller throughout the 1930s.

Gone to Earth was made into a film in 1950 and starred Jennifer Jones, a leading Hollywood actress of the time. In 1985 a restored version of the original film was issued by the National Film Archive to great acclaim and is now available on DVD.

Precious Bane was produced for BBC television in 1957 as a six part series, French television adapted it as a single drama episode in 1968 and in 1989 the BBC produced it as a play starring Clive Owen.

Mary Webb's style has influenced other great writers and Stella Gibbon's hugely successful novel *Cold Comfort Farm* has parallels with Mary Webb's work.

Mary Webb's contribution is recognised in the Tourist Information Centre in Much Wenlock, the Mary Webb School in Pontesbury, the Mary Webb Society, the Mary Webb Library at Bayston Hill. Several books about her life and work have been published. The revival of interest in her works began in earnest in the 1970s and continues today.

The home where she was truly happy, Spring Cottage at Bayston Hill, is still in existence but is now unrecognisable from Mary's happier days.

Like so many before her, Mary Webb was unable to enjoy the fruits of her labour during her own lifetime, but her fame increased long after her death.

Edith Pargeter 1913-1995

A television series that captured the imagination of viewers featured, unusually, a fictional 12th century detective, a Benedictine monk called Brother Cadfael from Shrewsbury Abbey. Starring Sir Derek Jacobi, the *Cadfael* series was based on the twenty or so medieval mystery novels written by Ellis Peters.

Ellis Peters was the pen name of Edith Pargeter who was born in Horsehay, Shropshire, on 28 September 1913. Educated at Dawley Church of England School and then Coalbrookdale High School for Girls, she started writing from around the age of seven, graduating from poems to articles for the school magazine as a teenager.

Although she had to undertake other work to earn a living, Edith was determined to become a writer and one of her first jobs working as a chemist's assistant provided invaluable background knowledge for her future plots.

Her first novel, *Hortensius, Friend of Nero* was published in 1936 to no great acclaim, although it was in fact the forerunner of a prolific writing career that would result in more than 90 publications! She also wrote articles for magazines to boost her income. In 1939, her second novel, *The City Lies Foursquare*, was more successful, giving an indication of what was to come.

The Second World War interrupted her career, like so many others, and Edith became a petty officer in the Wrens and was awarded the British Empire Medal for her dedication to duty. She continued to write during the war and her novel, *She Goes To War*, was based on her own experiences.

In 1947 this remarkable woman went to Czechoslovakia to work in a summer school and in very short time became so fluent in Czech that she could teach in the language and translate Czech poetry into English. For her services to Czech literature she was awarded the Gold Medal of the Czechoslovak Society for International Relations. Ever aware of her surroundings and observant of opportunities, she wrote *Fair Young Phoenix*, based on her experience at this time.

On her return to England she continued to write, using pseudonyms at times, but reserving the name Ellis Peters for her mystery novels. Her very first in this genre, *Fallen Into the Pit* was followed by her creation of the defining character of her career, Brother Cadfael, who she first featured in *A Morbid Taste for Bones* set in Shrewsbury Abbey around 1100.

The fictional Cadfael is an ex-soldier, a former crusader who turns to the church and is able, through his skills with ancient herbs and his experience of human psychology, to solve a whole range of crimes. Ellis Peters found the energy, skill and wit to produce 21 Cadfael-based mystery novels, throughout a period of 18 years. It was an amazing feat to maintain the popularity of a character over such a long time.

She was recognised in Britain by the Crime Writers' Association and the Mystery Writers of America, and also was awarded an OBE for her services to literature.

Edith Pargeter, aka Ellis Peters, died in 1995 aged 82, in Madeley, Shropshire where she had lived since 1956. In tribute to her, a stained glass window depicting St Benedict was installed in Shrewsbury Abbey in 1997.

Pargeter lived in Shropshire for most of her life and her stories invariably revolved around the county that she loved.

Barbara Pym *1913-1980*

Another of Shropshire's female writers to achieve national recognition was born in Willow Street, Oswestry in 1913. Brought up in affluent circumstances, her solicitor father ensured that she received a first class education, first of all at Liverpool College, Huyton, before going on to study English at St Hilda's, Oxford.

The family moved to Morda Lodge, a substantial Edwardian house on the outskirts of Oswestry, where Barbara was brought up in a church-going environment. Her father sang in the choir and her mother played the organ at the local parish church, St Oswald. Her parents were both devotees of opera and members of the Oswestry Operatic Society, so it was no surprise when Barbara's first significant work, encouraged by her mother, was an operetta, called *The Magic Diamond*. Exposure of this work extended only to home performances put on by family and friends, but Barbara was only eight years old when she wrote it!

Her literary career was suspended during World War II, so national recognition of her first published work, *Some Tame Gazelle*, only came in 1950. An eager public in 1952 were served up *Excellent Women*; in 1953, *Jane and Prudence*; 1955, *Less Than Angels*; 1958, *A Glass of Blessings*; and then in 1961; *No Fond Return of Love*.

During the permissive 1960s, Barbara Pym's popularity suddenly dipped. The publishers clamouring for her next work disappeared. An unexpected champion was at hand, however, and through his support, Pym's career was resurrected. Philip Larkin, one of England's greatest 20th century poets, was extremely fond of her work and said so. When, in 1977, Pym's novel *Quartet In Autumn* was published, it was greeted with acclaim and she once again became popular. A round of literary and publicity launches ensued, followed by the reissue of some of her works. In 1965 she had written *An Unsuitable Attachment*, though the manuscript was just gathering dust in her house. With her reputation re-established, this book was published in 1982, two years after her death. Two further novels, *A Few Green Leaves* in 1980 and *Crampton Hodnet* in 1985, were also published posthumously.

Barbara Pym had more than a dozen novels published and her gentle humour edged with a sadness endeared her to her fans to the extent that there is a Barbara Pym Society, established in 1994, and several books have been devoted to her life and works.

Percy Thrower *1913-1988*

Percy Thrower was not a Salopian by birth, but certainly by adoption, as his fame and fortune were very much established during his residence in the county.

During a recent survey, gardening was said to be the most favoured hobby in the British Isles and it is no exaggeration to suggest that it was Percy Thrower who was a leading figure behind this. For many years, the broadcaster, horticulturalist and writer was the face and the voice of British gardening, establishing for himself a national and international reputation.

He was born on 30 January 1913 at Horwood House, Milton Keynes, Buckinghamshire, where his father was the Head Gardener. Inspired by his father, he showed an early love and aptitude for gardening and after leaving school he spent four years working under his father learning the basics for his future career. At the age of 18 he left home and worked as a jobbing gardener at Windsor Castle where he lived in a small bothy earning £1 per week under Head Gardener, Charles Cook. After four years he moved to Leeds and joined the Parks and Gardens Department where he successfully passed his Royal Horticultural Society examinations.

Once again demonstrating his ambition by moving to Derby

in 1937, he spent eight years with the Parks Department during which time he passed the National Diploma in Horticulture, became a lecturer at Derby Technical College, and was eventually promoted to Assistant Parks Superintendent. He married Connie Cook, the daughter of his mentor, Charles Cook, at Windsor Castle. Charles had left Windsor and was working for Queen Mary at Sandringham and it was there that Percy and Connie were married on 9 September 1939. During the war years, Thrower was instrumental in the organisation of the 'Dig for Victory' campaign, encouraging the populace to grow their own food on even the smallest amount of land.

Fuelled once again by ambition, at the end of the war he moved to Shropshire where in 1946, at the age of 33, he became the youngest Parks Superintendent in the country when taking over at Shrewsbury, a post that he would hold for almost 30 years.

It was in 1951 that he first became exposed to the nation through the medium of television. The Shropshire Horticultural Society asked him to design an English-style garden for Berlin and he threw himself into the project with great enthusiasm. After it was completed it was opened by the Prime Minister, Anthony Eden, in May 1952. During the design stages and initial construction, the work was featured on television the previous year.

Shortly afterwards he started to receive invitations from the BBC to appear on radio programmes including *Beyond The Back Door*, which led to television appearances (in black and white) on *County Calendar* then *Out and About*. With the introduction of colour television, the concept of television gardening was greatly enhanced and *Gardeners' Club* blossomed with the public.

In the meantime, in Shrewsbury he was helping establish the county's reputation as the 'City of Flowers', and ensuring that the Shrewsbury Flower Show was one of the best in the country.

He was by now an instantly recognisable public face and his friendly, relaxed mannerisms, his beloved pipe and his catchphrase:

'the answer lies in the soil' resonated with the British public and he became a firm favourite.

In 1963 he bought a one-and-a-half acre site near the village of Bomere Heath, Shrewsbury, on which he built his house, The Magnolias. It would be the location for a number of *Gardeners' World* television shows and from 1966 it was opened to the public for charitable purposes.

The BBC appointed him to present *Gardeners' World* in 1969, which became a massive hit with the British public and he presented the programme until 1976 when the BBC cancelled his contract because he agreed to do a series of commercial advertisements for ICI. By now of course he was Britain's first celebrity gardener and consequently had a high profile and was a regular guest on chat shows. He wrote columns for the *Daily Mail*, the *Daily Express*, the *Sunday Express*, and *Amateur Gardening Magazine*. He had numerous books published. He was the inspiration for several of the next generation of television gardeners, particularly Alan Titchmarsh.

In 1969 he bought Hilda Murrell's garden business and established the *Percy Thrower Garden Centre*, employing his three daughters, Margaret born in 1944, Susan in 1948 and Ann in 1952, ensuring a loyal, dependable family business.

Percy remained much in demand and despite his problems with the BBC, he was invited in 1974 onto the children's hugely popular programme, *Blue Peter*. He promoted gardening as an interest and a hobby and also set up the Blue Peter Garden, which intrigued children for years as the seasons changed and the demands of the garden changed. Celebrities were invited to come along and were, from time to time, expected to work in the garden. Thrower's involvement with the Blue Peter Garden lasted until 1987 and involved an astonishing 100 appearances.

In 1974 Percy Thrower resigned as Shrewsbury Parks Superintendent after almost 30 years in the post, to pursue his very many other interests.

He lectured at the Royal Institution of Great Britain in 1976 on 'Changing Fashions in Gardening' and wrote his memoir, *My Lifetime in Gardening*, in 1977, the year in which the Royal Horticultural Society honoured him with their most prestigious award, the Victoria Medal of Honour.

His last few years were spent developing his Garden Centre near Shrewsbury, leading to a number of innovations: not only selling plants and dispensing advice but also selling garden furniture and pond liners, the forerunners of many of the ancillary items that today's garden centres all retail.

He was honoured with an MBE in 1984 but showed little sign of slowing down. He was hosting garden tours of Europe, lecturing on cruise ships and appearing at English Garden Weekends, until 1988, when he was taken ill during such a weekend. From his hospital bed he made what was to be his last recording for the *Blue Peter* programme. He died within the week.

He was buried on 18 March 1988 at Leaton Church near

Bronze tribute to Percy Thrower situated in the picturesque setting of the Dingle in The Quarry, Shrewsbury. Thrower held the position of Parks Superintendent for almost thirty years.

the village of Bomere Heath, Shropshire, where he had lived for almost 30 years.

In August 2005 his three daughters attended the unveiling of a bronze statue of their late father at the opening of the Shrewsbury Flower Show. It was situated on St Chad's Terrace overlooking the 30-acre showground site and was scheduled to have been unveiled by Percy's wife Connie, but sadly just weeks before the ceremony, Connie passed away at the age of 90. Following an act of vandalism, a bust of Percy Thrower has now been relocated at Shrewbury's The Dingle quarry.

His eldest daughter Margaret ran the Percy Thrower Garden Centre until it was taken over in 2000 by The Garden and Leisure Group.

In Brief

Other Salopians worthy of mention are:

• Sir Edward German, the Edwardian composer who was born in Whitchurch in 1862. Several of his light operas achieved national recognition, particularly '*Merrie England*' and '*Tom Jones*' but he was greatly honoured, as was the county of Shropshire, when he became the composer of the Coronation March and Hymn for King George V's Coronation in 1910.

• Hodnet man and rector at the local church there for fifteen years, Bishop Reginald Heber would later become the Bishop of Calcutta. He was also regarded as one of the Victorian's greatest hymn writers, composing in particular the memorable, *Holy, Holy, Lord God Almighty.*

• Another Shropshire man from very modest beginnings was Len Murray. He was born the son of a farm-worker in Hadley in 1922, was educated at Wellington Grammar School, and throughout his life he fought to preserve the rights of the working man. He rose through the ranks of the trade unionists to become General Secretary of the Trade Union Congress in 1973, a position he held until retiring in 1984. Len Murray was regarded by friend and foe as a decent, honest man who abided by his principles and who had a strong sense of social justice.

Unfortunately for him, his time in high office coincided with the rise of the Prime Minister Margaret Thatcher and her determination to break the stranglehold that she felt that the trade unions had on the country. Following the miners' strike in 1984, trade union power was effectively broken and Len Murray, realising that the trade unions had to adapt to a more realistic stance, retired.

His services to the Trade Union Congress and to the working men were recognised and he was appointed Lord Murray of Epping. He died in 2004.

Chapter Three

FASCINATING CHARACTERS

The previous chapter deals with Salopians who have made an outstanding contribution on the national and international stage. But Shropshire also boasts a diverse range of characters who have defied the norm! These include people who have contributed to the folklore and character of the county, with some truly amazing stories. Perhaps it is the constant struggle for survival that helped build Shropshire characters and create a defiant culture of not only survival, but also of success. The characters in this chapter all have that survival instinct and through their achievements and experiences, their stories, which have been handed down and perhaps embellished over the generations, have not only entertained their fellow Salopians, but also, in some cases, given inspiration.

Fulk Fitz Warin *1170-1260*
(Foulke, FitzWarren, Fitzwarine, FitzWaryn)

The legend of Robin Hood has long endured through the many stories of chivalry, derring-do and robbing of the rich to give to the poor. Even recvently, the BBC had a Robin Hood Saturday night television series which was as popular as ever. The historians however cannot come to a consensus as to whether he is fact or fiction or if indeed he is an amalgamation of several characters whose deeds are based on fact.

Over the centuries several locations have claimed to be the birthplace, or the stamping ground, of Robin Hood, with Nottingham usually emerging as favourite. It is believed that the first reference to Robin Hood was in a poem in 1377 based on exploits or deeds around the 13th century. Later stories, probably exaggerated to suit audiences, were then related by wandering minstrels travelling around the country, earning their living by singing tales. Perhaps that could be a reason for the various theories as to where Robin originated – it would make sense to impress an audience by locating the story in their own county.

There is compelling reason to believe that the legend of Robin Hood was based on the life of a Shropshire man, Fulk Fitz Warin. The British Museum has an old medieval French manuscript telling the story of the *Romance of Fouke le Fitz Warine* in English, Latin and French texts. A Middle English version was also produced.

The Fitz Warin family originated from Lorraine, arriving in this country to fight on the side of William the Conqueror, for which they were rewarded with land along the Wales-Shropshire border.

Fulk was born in 1170, and grew up with the Royal Princes, the future Kings, Richard the Lionheart and John I, in the court of Henry II. Legend has it that the young Fulk and John had a number of disagreements, leading to bad blood between them. Henry II was at this time trying to suppress the Welsh in a series of bloody battles and, after taking Whittington Castle in Oswestry, he gave it to his subject Roger Powys as a reward for his loyalty. The ownership of the castle had, for a number of years, been subject to claim and counterclaim.

Fulk returned home from the court of King Henry, and Richard the Lionheart left for the Crusades. In 1197 the Fulk family were named as the legal owners of Whittington Castle following a court judgement; the senior of the clan however died in 1198 before the family was able to take possession. Bad feeling between the Powys and the Fitz Warins erupted into a skirmish in 1200, in which Roger Powys' son Meurig was killed by a young Fulk Fitz Warin.

Remembering their past differences, King John had no hesitation in declaring the Fitz Warins as outlaws. The brothers took to the forests along the Welsh Border with a considerable number of followers and waged a guerrilla campaign. Fulk and his gang had no quarrel with the local people and indeed received considerable support from them. Stories abound of how the Fitz Warins policed the forests, ambushing rich merchants, showing them hospitality then relieving them of some of their possessions before helping them on their way. Some of the stories are no doubt apocryphal, particularly the tale that they captured King John while he was hunting in Windsor Forest, let him go when he agreed to pardon them, only to have him renege on the agreement.

After three years of roaming the forests, King John pardoned the Fitz Warin family and once again they returned, this time legitimately, to take over Whittington Castle. The pardon citation mentioned the Fitz Warins in particular, and 52 others, so it was a sizeable band of outlaws.

In 1207 Fulk Fitz Warin married Maude, daughter of Sir Robert le Vavasour on 1 October in York.

The impressive Gatehouse Towers of Whittington Castle, near Oswestry.

For a time Fulk was loyal to King John but matters came to a head in 1215 when John was forced into signing the Magna Carta. However the Welsh were on the attack again and soon after, they took over Whittington Castle. After the death of King John in 1216, Henry III defeated the rebel barons and the Welsh prince Llywelyn made peace with Henry. In 1220 Henry returned Whittington Castle, or what was left of it, to the Fitz Warins who began a rebuilding programme. Meanwhile, the struggle with the Welsh continued until 1239 when Llywelyn married Fulk's daughter.

There is a further magnificent, romantic Arthurian link to Fulk Fitz Warin and the Robin Hood legend. Near Albertbury, Fulk had built a structure called the White Abbey as a final resting place for his wife and a mysterious Holy Relic. There were rumours that Fulk was in possession of the Holy Grail, the cup of the Last Supper. However, he was convinced that what he had was the Marian Chalice, a small sacred ointment jar that had belonged to Mary Magdalene, which she had used to anoint Christ's body.

71

The Marian Chalice was said to have travelled to Britain and had last been seen with the Romans at Wroxeter.

In 1855 a descendant of Fulk Fitz Warin, a Shropshire writer Thomas Wright, claimed to have the Marian Chalice in his possession but no heirs to leave it to. He therefore decided to hide the object and to leave a poem full of clues to help direct those determined to find it. So obtuse and clever was the coding that no one had a clue how to find it until the 1990s.

Graham Philips, a writer himself, spent a long time researching the subject, studying the poem, *Sir Gawain and the Red Knight*. After many painstaking, frustrating days, he happened to crack the code. He discovered that the clues were all connected to Psalms and Bible numbers. Meticulously he followed the trail from the White Castle, to the Red Castle by a white cliff, into the caves of Shropshire's Hawkstone Park, coming out into the valley and down into the parish church at Hodnet. He stood in the tiny church contemplating his next move and realised that he had made a wrong turning and retraced his steps back to the caves where there had been a couple of statues. He deduced that the vessel was in the base of a statue of an eagle. To his utter despair he found that it had been broken open.

Undaunted, he discovered that the man who had taken the statues away, local builder Walter Langham, was now deceased. Phillips traced Langham's living relatives to Rugby, where they told him that Walter had found the tiny vessel and believed that it was an egg cup. To his great joy they also told Philips that it was still in their possession and they allowed him to handle it. It was a small stone vessel about the size and shape of an egg cup and made from green alabaster. The British Museum confirmed that it was a Roman ointment or scent jar dating from the first century and could well be the famed Marian Chalice. After almost 2,000 years, it had finally been traced thanks to the superb work of Graham Philips.

Fulk Fitz Warin had been blind for the last seven years of his life when he died in 1260 and his son Fulk Fitz Warin IV acted for his father in his last years.

Many connections, then, to Robin Hood: outlaws in the forest, Richard the Lionheart, King John, disputes over lands, a pardon. There is another possible link. Fulk was clearly very fond of his wife Maud and his second greatest possession was the Marian Chalice. Is it possible that the minstrels merged Maud and Marian to come up with Maid Marian?

Today all that is left of the once-magnificent Whittington Castle that formed part of the Marcher defences and was much fought over, is the gatehouse and two towers (reconstructed). At its zenith when owned by the Fitz Warins in the early 13th century until the 1330s, it had five stone towers and was surrounded by a moat; it was a formidable fortress. Fulk Fitz Warin VI and his wife modified the fortress and created a magnificent home with the centrepiece a scented herb garden. Unusually, the ruins today are owned by the local community and held in a Trust. They organise several events there annually and preserve the site for the benefit of their community and for the pleasure of visitors.

Dick Whittington 1350-1423

Another enduring folklore figure with a Shropshire link: Dick Whittington was an orphan from a very poor background who ran away to London carrying with him his possessions wrapped in a handkerchief suspended from a pole over his shoulder. His only companion was his famous cat. The seasonal pantomime version tells us that he ran away from home because he thought that the streets of London were paved with gold.

It is generally believed that the hero of this story is a certain Richard Whittington who came from Gloucester. He did indeed set out for London but he certainly wasn't poor: he was the son of Sir William Whittington, Lord of the Manor of Pauntley. But it was Richard's brother who was going to inherit the family estate and that is why the story has him setting out for London.

Once there, Dick had a difficult time finding work and was about to leave the city when, according to legend, the Bow Bells started to ring as he was leaving and they seemed to call to him 'Turn again, Whittington, thrice Mayor of London'.

He decided to stay and temporarily work as a scullery boy for the wealthy Fitzwarren family. The basis for Dick's fortune, according to legend, was his cat. A wealthy captain, whose ship, moored in London, was being over-run with rats, was desperate to clear them out and Dick loaned them his cat for the purpose. The cat quickly cleared the ship of all the rats and the grateful merchant paid Dick handsomely.

Dick married Alice Fitzwarren, daughter of Sir Ivo Fitzwarren and by the time of his death in 1423 Dick's achievements were considerable; he had become a successful and wealthy merchant, an MP for the city, and Lord Mayor of London on several occasions. His was truly the classic rags-to-riches story. He had wisely and generously used his wealth to benefit others, providing a drainage system for London, hospital wards for unmarried mothers and he played a prominent part in the well-being of the citizens of London.

Most of these facts are historically correct, but of course as with all good stories, embellishments are inevitable. Historically there is no evidence to support the notion of Dick having a pet cat which was the origin of his wealth.

However, Shropshire has a very good claim to be the home of the real Dick Whittington and here it is. He was the son of a local blacksmith born and brought up in a small village, The Newnes, near Ellesmere. The family fell under the influence of local vicar Roger de Hampton who saw potential in the young Whittington; the Knights Hospitaller, whose centre was at nearby

Halston, financially supported Hampton. After grooming young Dick and receiving the consent of his father, Hampton sent Dick to serve at the Head Quarters of the Knights of St John, at Clerkenwell, London.

In terms of the story, if Whittington served the very powerful Knights well and loyally, they would certainly have had the connections and the authority to form the basis of his later success.

There is also one other amazing coincidence. If the real Dick Whittington was, alternatively, from Gloucester, and married Alice Fitzwarren, then at the time of their marriage the Fitzwarrens owned Whittington Castle in North Shropshire! One would imagine that the Shropshire Dick Whittington would have known Alice as a neighbour.

The 14th century 'Dick Whittington Cottage' is at The Newnes, Ellesmere, adjacent to the Newnes Touring Caravan Park, on land previously owned by the Duke of Westminster. The cottage is now privately owned and has been renovated and re-thatched; restored from its almost derelict state, although it is believed to still have some of the original timbers.

As is so often the case with legends, this one is full of confusion. Dick Whittington from Gloucester? 'Oh no he wasn't!' From Shropshire? 'Oh yes he was!'

Sir Humphrey Kynaston 1474-1534
'Wild Man'

A jumbled pile of rubble is all that remains of a once-impressive tower set in the centre of a farm field in the village of Myddle. This is all that remains of Myddle Castle, the family seat of one of Shropshire's most amazing characters.

Born in 1474, although one respected chronicler claims that he was born in 1468, Humphrey Kynaston was the first son from Sir Roger Kynaston's second marriage, to Elizabeth Grey. From his first marriage to Mariona ap Griffiths, he had a son, who died in infancy, and a daughter.

So, when his father died, Humphrey inherited Myddle Castle but his recklessness and irresponsibility resulted in his lands and castle falling into disrepair. He was said to have been of a 'wild' temperament with little regard for reputation or person.

Heavily in debt, his truculence went too far one cold winter's day in 1491. He was out riding with Thomas Kynaston (his half brother) and Robert Hopton, when they encountered John Hughes.

The men, apparently unprovoked, attacked and killed the unfortunate Hughes: Humphrey stuck his lance into him, Thomas Kynaston hit him on the head with his sword and Hopton struck the man in the leg with a billhook. The three appeared in court on 20 December 1491 and were unable or unwilling to explain why they had attacked and murdered Hughes. They were found guilty.

Shortly after the trial and before he could be incarcerated, Humphrey fled his crumbling Myddle Castle, leaving behind his family and enormous debts; he was subsequently declared an outlaw by King Henry VII and his legend began.

He retreated into the wilds and settled in a cave in Nesscliffe Rock, close by the village of Nesscliffe. The approach to the cave is heavily wooded and up a very steep pathway, the end of which

76

leads to towering red sandstone cliffs. Set in the cliffside is the cave, which is spacious and divided into two sections by a pillar of stone. Here Humphrey Kynaston lived in one part, and his precious horse and sole companion, Beelzebub, lived in the other part. There is a path leading to the cave, which is accessed by steep stone steps. A heavy iron door guards the entrance. Today it is a protected historical site and is a real delight for those familiar with the story.

The horse would graze in the fields of amiable neighbours close by the hideout and would come whenever Kynaston whistled. His neighbours respected his secrecy and gave him food from time to time, while his horse was well provided-for and stabled. In return, Kynaston shared some of the spoils of his activities as a highwayman. Situated as he was, he could see the road winding between Shrewsbury and Oswestry from the top of Nesscliffe Hill,

The entrance to Kynaston's Cave: 26 steep stone steps leading to an iron door in the rock-face.

perfect for targeting the coaches and the carts of merchants bearing wool, silver, gold or grain.

His activities of course aroused indignation in others and several attempts were made to capture him. Stories of his exploits, many of course apocryphal, only added glamour to his reputation. The sheriff on one occasion laid an ambush for him and removed several planks from the bridge leading to his cave. Humphrey spotted the trap and spurred Beelzebub into a gallop so that she cleared the bridge in one leap. On another occasion the horse allegedly leapt 40ft across the River Severn to escape capture!

Another story demonstrated Kynaston's ruthlessness. He walked into his favourite inn, the *Three Pigeons* at Nesscliffe, which sits at the foot of the cliff, and took offence when he saw a man sitting in his favourite seat by the fireplace. Without further ado

The outlaw's favourite seat inside the fireplace of the Three Pigeons pub at Nesscliffe.

drew his pistol and shot him dead; he escaped by climbing up the chimney, out onto the roof and away. Perhaps the locals protected him out of a combination of respect and fear.

The pub today is said to have Humphrey's seat from his time in the Nesscliffe cave, carved out of the large fireplace as a sandstone cleft.

In later life Humphrey was pardoned. He may have accumulated a good deal of wealth from his highwayman proceeds because on 16 June 1513, as the English army moved into France, a banner was upheld with the words, Shrop-Homffray Kynaston and Thomas Trentham, under which Standard, 100 men were marching. For his support and loyalty Henry VIII pardoned him in around 1516.

Sir Humphrey Kynaston married again, this time Isabella, and they had four children between 1515 and 1519. He died in 1534, some say in the cave at Nesscliffe, others that he died in Welshpool. However, his will stated that all his land and tenements in England and Wales should go to his eldest son Edward, except the property and land of Knockyn which should go to his younger son Roger. Such a legacy hardly befits the profile of a cave dweller.

A remarkable man, who moved from riches to rags and through crime, back to riches and respectability, with a reputation as the 15th century Dick Turpin.

Thomas Parr 1483-1635
'Old Tom Parr'

Shropshire's Thomas Parr was said to be the oldest man ever to have lived in Britain or indeed virtually anywhere else. For those who believe his story, he was born in a cottage at The Glyn near Wollaston in 1483. As a boy he served at Rowton Castle which today is a private hotel, before around 1500 spending some time in the army. However after the death of his father he returned to the family cottage to take up the remaining years on the lease.

He first married at the age of 80 and fathered two children who sadly died in infancy and according to the stories handed down, he had an affair when he was 100, resulting in an illegitimate child and when he was 122 he married for the second time!

At the age of 152 in 1635 he was something of a celebrity and would have lived through the reigns of no less than ten monarchs. Thomas Howard, the Earl of Arundel, thought his longevity worthy of an audience with King Charles I who it was said was brusque and almost dismissive of the old man. During their meeting Charles asked him what he had done to place himself above other long-lived men. Tom replied that he was the oldest man to have performed penance (following his affair). However worse, much worse, was to come.

Thomas Parr had become over many years used to a regime of rest and a strict vegetarian diet in the healthy open countryside. The wining and dining and the total change of environment and the continual questions from people anxious to meet this curiosity had a disastrous effect on Old Tom. He was taken ill in London and what was supposed to be a joyous celebration of his great age turned to tragedy when he died on 14 November 1635. The post-mortem on his body was carried out by Dr William Hervey, the physician to the King, and afterwards Hervey opined that Old Tom Parr was nearer to 70 than 152!

Nevertheless King Charles generously allowed him to be buried in Westminster Abbey on 15 November 1635 and the gravestone inscription that is still visible today notes his life span and lists the names of the monarchs he was alleged to have survived.

He has been commemorated in poems and books: Dickens' *Dombey & Son* and in Bram Stoker's *Dracula*. Old Tom Parr has been featured on American television, *Beyond Belief*, and his name has been linked with a whole range of health-giving products as well as a Scotch whisky, *Old Parr*, named after him. In addition to all that, Rubens and Van Dyke painted his portrait. He was a national celebrity.

The doubters believe that Tom Parr's records may well have become confused with those of his grandfather, but there is no concrete evidence to disprove Shropshire's Old Tom Parr's claim to being Britain's longest living person.

Judge Sir George Jeffreys 1648-1689 *'The Hanging Judge'*

One of the most notorious and infamous characters of British history, George Jeffreys, had a tenuous link with Shropshire but nevertheless his early education and his late choice of a baronetcy associate him with the county.

He was born in Wrexham on 15 May 1648 and in 1652 was enrolled at Shrewsbury School, the old school of his grandfather who was a judge in North Wales. He was tutored by a friend of his mother's at Shrewsbury School where one of his contemporaries was William Wycherley, later to become a Restoration dramatist and a person who would feature in Jeffreys' later life. In 1659 Jeffreys left Shrewsbury to go on to St Paul's school and from there to Cambridge University.

After leaving Cambridge without graduating, he began to study law in the Inner Temple and was soon acting as an advocate before being officially called to the Bar and entering Gray's Inn. His rise was nothing short of meteoric. He was knighted in 1677, became the Recorder of London in 1678 at the age of 30 and by the time he was 35, his honours embraced Lord Chief Justice of England, Privy Counsellor and, in 1685, Lord Chancellor.

In 1684 King James II awarded Jeffreys a baronetcy for his

loyalty and service. It so happened that Daniel Wycherley, the father of William Wycherley, was preparing to sell the manors of Wem and Loppington. Wem at the time was a small market town with several surrounding hamlets including Wolverley and Aston with a number of large houses. Historical records reveal that Jeffreys paid Wycherley £9,000 for the baronetcy and Sir George Jeffreys became the Ist Baron of Wem.

Despite his enormous success and acclaim, his private life was far from happy. His first wife Sarah Neesham, whom he had married when they were both in their early twenties, gave him five sons and two daughters and they had a very happy marriage. When she died aged 34, he was devastated. He was also plagued for most of his life by kidney and bladder stones which frequently caused him great pain and he would resort to alcohol to give him a degree of relief, earning him the reputation of being a drunkard. Certainly, if any poor unfortunate came before him when he was suffering an attack from his painful stones, then his reputation of being merciless and cold seemed well-earned.

Jeffreys has been remembered in history for the aftermath of the Duke of Monmouth's Rebellion in 1685, when Monmouth and his followers rose up against James II and were decisively defeated at the Battle of Sedgemoor. Monmouth was caught and executed and Jeffreys was appointed to lead four other judges who visited the West Country: Winchester, Dorchester, Taunton and Wells, to carry out the trials of those suspected of supporting the rebellion, in a series of actions recorded in history as the 'Bloody Assizes'.

In the first high-profile case in Winchester, Dame Alice Lyle, an elderly refined lady, was found guilty and was sentenced to be burned at the stake. In an act regarded as charitable at the time, her sentence was commuted and she was beheaded in Winchester market place!

In Taunton, despite the pleas of the Mayor who knew an accused man to be innocent, Jeffreys went ahead and had him hanged shortly before he was pardoned. Judge Jeffreys shouted at and berated an eight-year old girl so much that she fainted in the courtroom and later died of fright.

It is estimated that 1,400 prisoners were brought before the judges, presided over by Judge Jeffreys. Most were sentenced to death although only around 300 were actually executed in the barbaric process of hanging, drawing and quartering. Over 1,000 of those sentenced to death were reprieved and instead transported to the West Indies and sold into slavery. Many prisoners awaiting trial contracted typhus and other terminal diseases and died in the interim.

The corpses of the executed as a result of the Monmouth Rebellion were left hanging, as an example to others, exposed to the elements and to wildlife. It was said that Jeffreys sometimes attended the executions and would stand quietly observing. He once sentenced the serial offender, Titus Oates, to a most brutal public thrashing in which the victim collapsed on several occasions but was then revived and the thrashing continued unabated.

At the end of the 'Bloody Assizes', Jeffreys returned to London and James II rewarded him for his dedication to duty with the appointment of Lord Chancellor!

However within three years, rebellion was once again re-surfacing and James II was forced to flee to France. Jeffreys, with gold coins secreted about his person, was pursued as he too tried to escape, knowing that many people had a score to settle with him as the bloodthirsty 'Hanging Judge'. Luckily for Jeffreys he was captured by soldiers and locked in the Tower for his own safety. Just a year later he died in the Tower of the kidney/bladder diseases that had haunted him for much of his life. His dying wish was to be buried next to his first wife and children and her death may well have been the catalyst for his subsequent ruthless decisions.

One of his sons inherited the baronetcy and although his father had never actually stayed there, his son did visit and stay in Shropshire at Lowe Hall, Wem, in the house that still stands today.

Molly Morgan 1762-1835
'Queen of the Hunter Valley'

On the other side of the world, two hours north of Sydney, Australia, and 12,000 miles from Shropshire, is the small town of Maitland, the gateway to the beautiful Hunter Valley, one of the largest wine producing areas of Australia.

The town is picturesque, with small streets lined with shops and restaurants complementing its oldest buildings dating from the 18th century. Antique shops, heritage walks and tours to the nearby vineyards reflect the pride that the modern townsfolk have in their history. One of the Hunter Valley wineries is called Molly Morgan and is overlooked by Molly Morgan Ridge. Tourists travelling on the New England Highway pass the Molly Morgan Motor Inn. Unsurprisingly, the place names reflect the name of the founder of the town, but more surprisingly, the founder was Shropshire born and bred in the beautiful village of Diddlebury!

Her incredible story has all the ingredients required for a modern blockbuster movie. History does not relate how physically attractive Molly was, but to have survived her many ordeals, she quite clearly must have used her feminine wiles to good effect.

She was born Mary Jones in a tiny cottage behind the Crofton, Diddlebury on 31 January 1762 to David and Margaret Jones. She went to the local school, today's Corvedale CofE primary school, and on leaving, took up needlework, and that wasn't all she took up for, at the age of 21, she gave birth to an illegitimate son. In 1785 she married wheelwright William Morgan from Hopesay, giving birth to another son the following year when they moved to Cold Weston.

In 1788 the landlord of the *Sun Inn* discovered that a supply of yarn that he had put aside for bleaching had gone missing. The Morgans were linked to its disappearance by reputation, and when their property was searched, the yarn was found. They were arrested but William managed to escape and Molly, while locked up in the *Sun Inn* overnight, tried to kill herself by cutting her throat. In those days justice was severe and theft of goods valued at more than one shilling was punishable by death! The yarn was valued at £4 so Molly was well aware of the punishment to come. She was sentenced to death but it was commuted to 14 years transportation in the colonies: in Molly's case, Australia.

The sea voyage itself was in those days a death sentence for many and for women, particularly the more attractive ones, survival depended very much on their compliance with the sexual demands of the officers. The ship, *The Neptune*, was a former slave trader that had been fitted out for transporting convicts. More than 500 convicts chained together were crammed below decks into cages 6' x 6', ten to a cage, in a space below decks no bigger than a tennis court. Starved, abused, with little exercise and subject to disease, it was no wonder that on this particular voyage 158 died and of the 344 survivors reaching Port Jackson, 269 had to be carried ashore, so weakened were they by vermin and disease: Molly survived and, according to some accounts, survived well!

Amazingly her husband eventually joined her in Australia after either committing a new offence or, more likely, being caught for the original theft. Molly was awarded a ticket-of-leave and she and her husband William opened a shop in Parramatta but after a time she became bored with him, and after five years in the colony, she made plans to escape back to England.

She befriended Captain Locke of the *Resolution* who, after succumbing to her charms, smuggled her aboard and assisted her escape from Australia. One account suggests that, in return for her safe passage, Molly promised to marry the captain but, once safely back in England she reneged on her promise. Molly was certainly courageous, as the very act of escaping from the colony was an offence punishable by death.

In England, resourceful as ever, Molly ensnared a wealthy brass founder from Plymouth and entered into a bigamous marriage with him. For a time they were happy but after a serious quarrel Molly burnt down their house and her 'husband' reported her crime to the authorities. She was also accused of the theft of several small linen articles and, after being found guilty of arson, she was again sentenced to be deported for seven years to Australia.

Once again she faced the four month sea voyage in horrendous circumstances but landed safely in 1804. Her feminine wiles quickly ensnared an army captain and after they married, they settled down with some land and a few head of cattle. For a time they were happy, the farm prospered and their herd of cattle multiplied at an impressive rate – so much so that it attracted the attention of neighbours and government officials. It was then discovered that Molly had been stealing cattle and branding them with her own brand. In 1814 she was therefore sentenced to seven years in the harsh settlement regions for offenders at Newcastle Penal Colony.

Using her charms she was granted permission in 1819 to move with a party of settlers to a new region (now Maitland) and soon set up home with one of the officers of the settlement. After he used his influence, she obtained parole and a Crown Land Grant of 159 acres at Wallis Plains, an area which would eventually form the basis of today's modern city of Maitland, a major centre of the Hunter Valley region. Her capacity for hard work was matched by her ingenuity and she quickly established a reputation for building fences, digging ditches, constructing dams, riding and shooting. She claimed that she was a match for any man.

On Wallis Plains she opened the first, primitive tavern and very quickly built up a network of similar ones along the river ports and bullock transport sectors. She was of course dealing in the liquor trade but it was illegal to supply convicts with liquor and convicts made up the main work force in the region and were her main source of customers. Molly was, true to form, undaunted by this, and as the mistress of one of the local officials, she got away without being prosecuted. In 1823 and at the age of 61, Molly married for the fourth time, this time to a much younger man. One assumes that men of her own age were unable to cope with her!

Molly's later years were filled with success, not only in her personal life but also in her efforts towards those less fortunate than herself. *The Australian*, in 1827, published a tribute to Molly Hunt (Morgan) praising her donations towards the building of the local school and church. She established a hospital, assisted settlers on arrival, helped during a flood crisis and worked unstintingly for the improved welfare of convicts.

One story told how at the age of 61 she rode on horseback all the way to Sydney to save the lives of some convicts wrongly accused of stealing fruit, the injustice of their situation stirring her into action.

In the region around Wallis Plain, known to the locals as Molly Morgan Plains, she was renowned and respected.

True, she seldom respected the laws of the land, any land. She was fearless, determined and some might say ruthless with her emotions, and perhaps prostituted herself to survive or thrive. Nevertheless, to have been convicted and sent to Australia twice, to have endured the horrors of two four-month journeys on death ships, subjected to the whims of officers; to have survived a further guilty verdict in Australia and then to have built a successful life on the back of unbelievable adversity, underlines the fact that Molly Morgan was a most exceptional person.

At the time of her death in 1835 at the age of 73, this Shropshire lady was known to all as the Queen of the Hunter Valley and was much respected and mourned by all who knew her.

John Mytton 1796-1834
'Mad Jack'

'Mad' Jack Mytton came from a wealthy family of landed Shropshire squires whose family seat was Halston Hall at Whittington, Oswestry. His ancestors and his peer group were aristocratic, privately educated and followed the traditional route of their class and breeding with a career at officer level in the army before using their wealth and influence to gravitate to politics and become Members of Parliament for their local constituency. This normal career path was followed almost to the letter by John Mytton.

His education had been a disaster, revealing the traits that would dominate the rest of his life. He was expelled in his first year at Westminster School for fighting, before moving on to Harrow where he broke some kind of record by being expelled after three days! His desperate family then had him tutored privately but he treated his tutors with disdain.

His family clearly used their influence to get him into Cambridge University despite his appalling record. It is believed that he arrived there with 2,000 bottles of port wine to help him, he claimed, to overcome the boredom of study; and he left without graduating. Like most spoilt wealthy young rakes of the time, he then decided to broaden his horizons and embarked on a tour of Europe.

After that the only avenue left open to him was the army and he joined the 7th Hussars and spent a year in occupied France as a young Cornet officer, following the defeat of Napoleon. Once again he became bored, spending most of his time gambling and drinking until he resigned. He was aware, of course, that at the age of 21 he would inherit his father's estate and the certainty of being wealthy for life clearly had a detrimental effect on his ambitions for the future.

His father had died at the age of 30 when Jack was only two, but when Jack reached his 21ˢᵗ birthday he inherited the family estate and a considerable fortune. Estimates place the property in today's valuation at over £4 million and the annual income inherited by Jack is equivalent to £700,000 today! Jack was, by any stretch of the imagination, a very wealthy young man.

In 1819 at the age of 23 he bought his way into Parliament after encouraging the locals to vote for him by donating to each supporter a £10 note. He spent an estimated three quarters of a million pounds at today's valuation, to secure the role of Member of Parliament for Shrewsbury. However, as a young man his temperament was unsuited for responsibility and he found Parliament boring, attending the House of Parliament only once.

In 1818 Jack had married a Baronet's daughter, but she tragically died two years later and this may have made Jack reckless of his own safety, although some say that he treated her very badly, as he did his second wife, Caroline Giffard. He had children from both marriages but behaved in a wild fashion with them. There was also a rumour that he tried to push Caroline into Halston

The entrance to Jack Mytton's ancestral home of Halston Hall at Whittington, Oswestry. The hall remains today a private dwelling.

Lake and once locked her in with his foxhounds; unsurprisingly Caroline ran away in 1830.

Very quickly Jack turned his attention to other pursuits and at last found something he was good at: horse racing and gambling. It was a bet in 1826 that led to one of his legendary exploits. Jack rode a horse into the *Bedford Hotel* opposite the Town Hall in Leamington Spa, spurred it up the grand staircase and onto the balcony overlooking part of the dining hall. Pausing for a moment to contemplate his next move and watched open-mouthed by the diners below, he suddenly kicked the horse into action and it leaped off the balcony over the heads of the petrified diners below and galloped through the open window out onto the parade. Bravado? Madness? Irresponsible? All of those and more.

He was a first class horseman, daring and fearless, and was particularly fond of fox hunting. He would not be put off the chase, irrespective of weather conditions. He at times appeared totally oblivious to the cold, riding in the depths of winter in garments usually reserved for the summer and sometimes he rode naked. He would roll around naked in snowdrifts and swim rivers swollen with winter ice and once he completed a full day's hunt after sustaining broken ribs, when every jolt must have been agony. He was spending money at an alarming rate and it was said that at one time he had 150 pairs of hunting breeches, 700 pairs of handmade hunting boots, 1,000 hats and 3,000 shirts.

He also had a penchant for dogs and around the manor at any one time there were an estimated 2,000 dogs, including foxhounds, gun dogs, pointers and retrievers. His treatment of his dogs and horses bordered on the bizarre: the dogs would be fed on steak and champagne and sometimes he dressed them in livery. One of his horses, Baronet, had the freedom to wander around Halston Hall and would often sprawl in front of the fire with its master. But despite his seeming love of his animals, one night he forced the death of one of his favourite horses by getting it to drink a bottle of port.

His antics often suggested a death wish. He would lie between the hooves of volatile horses, almost inviting injury; he drove his carriage deliberately at a hole to see if it would turn over. He surpassed that by driving his coach and horses full pelt at a tollgate to see if it could clear. It couldn't, but he escaped unscathed.

At times his antics were more mischievous than malicious but still sometimes caused great anxiety and upset, particularly the night when he invited to dinner a local vicar and doctor. After a good evening of dining and drinking, his guests left on horseback: Jack donned a highwayman's outfit and, arming himself with pistols, took a short cut and caught up with his guests. Bursting from cover he pursued the terrified men shooting his pistols over their heads. He terrified dinner guests one night at Halston Hall when he rode into the dining room dressed in full hunting gear on a bear. When he put the spur into the bear it turned and sank its teeth into his leg in front of the alarmed guests. He kept the bear as a pet for some time but was forced to have it put down when it attacked one of his servants.

His servants, tenants and workmen found him to be fair and generous and loved Jack: he paid his servants well. He often spent time eating at the homes of his tenants who would treat him to full fat bacon and quarts of ale around a roaring open fire and then he would stagger back to the Hall where his servants had prepared a full dinner.

Jack was of course not the conventional, aloof aristocrat and the ordinary locals had a certain admiration for him. There was one occasion when a tough Shropshire miner had interfered with Jack's hunting and after sharp words were exchanged, the dispute developed into a full fist -fight. After 20 rounds of brutal blows, it was the miner who was forced to admit defeat.

Despite his love for his dogs, he was an aficionado of dog fighting and would gamble on the outcome. He was also said to take his fists to his own bulldog and is supposed to have raised a mastiff into the air by grasping it in his own jaws and standing upright unaided. He is even supposed to have put Caroline's pet dog on an open fire whilst in a temper!

Jack was spending money as if there were no tomorrow and, after averaging eight bottles of port wine with a dash of brandy each day, there were few tomorrows in sight. Friends and advisers continually warned him that his fortune was running out and his agent told him that if he could reduce his annual spending to £6,000 per annum (around £450,000 by today's valuation) the estate would not have to be sold. Hardly a massive sacrifice but Jack retorted, 'I wouldn't give a damn to live on £6,000 a year.'

The creditors were closing in and shortly after Caroline left in 1830, Jack fled to France to avoid his debts, court and almost certainly prison.

Just before crossing the channel he met a young lady, Susan, and charmed her with the promise of £500 per annum to be his companion in France.

There was one final mad escapade in France when Jack, annoyed by hiccups, set his shirt on fire with a lighted candle believing that it would frighten the 'hiccups' away. The flames quickly engulfed his cotton nightshirt and he was saved from very serious burns by the intervention of his friend, Charles Apperley.

As they beat out the flames Jack yelled out 'the hiccup is gone, by God.'

The following morning, Apperley recorded in his book, (eventually published under the title of *The Memoirs of the Life of the Late John Mytton*) that when he went to Mytton's room, his skin had come off in sheets, leaving him with the appearance of a singed piece of bacon!

Within two years, Mytton had returned to England to face the music and was sent to the King's Bench debtor's prison in Southwark where in 1834 he died penniless, almost friendless, his health destroyed by alcohol and earlier gluttony. He ended his life the ghost of the energetic, confident daredevil young man who once had the world at his feet.

For one who died so young, it is remarkable that Jack Mytton's reputation lives on today. Charles Apperley, writing as 'Nimrod', wrote a series of articles about his friend's life and exploits for the *New Sporting Magazine*. Today when the originals come up at auction, they fetch thousands of pounds.

Shropshire has a number of place names in the county, lanes, streets and roads bearing his name and he is also commemorated in the Jack Mytton Way, a 72-mile route especially suited to walkers and cyclists traversing mid-Shropshire.

At the village of Hindford is the *Jack Mytton Pub* and just down the lane is the impressive entrance to his old family seat, Halston Hall, now a private residence.

On the day of his funeral, the procession on its way to Halston Chapel paused at an inn at Atcham close by the River Severn. The hotel is now called *The Mytton & Mermaid* and one of its bars is called *Mad Jack's Bar*.

His name is even commemorated in America in a way that would bring a smile of approval to his face. The University of Minnesota, Minneapolis, instigated in 1999 what has become an annual event, The Jack Mytton Run, a nude student streak from the university campus up to the Northrup Mall on the first day following the spring break.

Jack Mytton would have approved: indeed he probably would have organised it!

The sign of the Mytton & Mermaid hotel at Atcham, the site of the Halston Inn at which 'Mad' Jack Mytton's funeral cortege paused for drinks.

93

Chapter Four

MEN OF THE CLOTH

We have done those things which we ought not to have done

Imagine an author anxiously placing his latest manuscript before a prospective publisher.

Author: 'I think you'll like it. It's got fraud, vindictiveness, a feud, sex, a peeping Tom and adultery.'

Editor: 'Sounds promising. Anything else?'

Author: 'Well, yes, there's a murder and a hanging.'

Editor: 'Who's the murderer?'

Author: 'The local vicar.'

Editor: 'The local vicar? No, no come on. That's too far-fetched: we need to be more realistic. Readers will quickly realise that the story's too contrived. No, sorry, won't do.'

It is often said that the truth is stranger than fiction and sadly the above story is far from fiction and accurately outlines the events that took place in the small Shropshire parish of Stanton Lacy, just two miles north of Ludlow, in the 17th century.

This fertile area, with plentiful water from the rivers, has yielded evidence of settlement and organised farming dating back 5,000 years and has burial mounds from the Bronze Age. Archaeologists have unearthed evidence of a Roman villa in the village and the Saxons came to the area around the tenth century and built the village church, St Peter's, around which the tragic events are centred.

In the early 1600s the population of Stanton Lacy was a thriving 400 or so, and the village embraced around 7,000 acres of top quality farmland.

In May 1639 a new vicar, Thomas Atkinson, whose patron was Lord John Craven, arrived in the village; he was also the rector at Wistanstow. Around 1645 Atkinson married for a second time and through this marriage became related to the Cravens. In 1648 Lord Craven died and was succeeded by his brother William Craven who inherited great wealth. Reverend Atkinson became William's chaplain as well as a relative and friend. However William was a soldier and a Royalist and when the Civil War came to Ludlow and the Parliamentarians routed the Royalists, William Craven was forced into exile.

Atkinson was condemned by association. He was allowed to return to his vicarage in 1651 but of course had lost the patronage and funding from William Craven who was still abroad and whose estates had been confiscated. Parliament also removed from him the rectory at Wistanstow. He was now forced to live in the village in much reduced circumstances, depending on tithes from the parishioners and on fees for baptisms, burials and marriages. However, the tithes arrangement had never been updated and for many years had remained as a fixed sum which now bore little comparison to true values. Tithe disputes were a regular occurrence and source of irritation. Atkinson was also forced to take a tenant into the farmhouse that he leased, to help supplement his income.

It is believed that he married for a third time around 1653 after his second wife Ann died, although there is no record of her burial. She may well have died in giving birth to daughter Ann in 1650.

Political pressure and the stress and strain of struggling to survive whilst preaching the virtues of religion undermined his health and in 1657, at the age of 53, Reverend Thomas Atkinson passed away, leaving a widow, Elizabeth, two sons and a daughter.

In 1661, the two boys were sent to Christ Church, Oxford to be educated, one eventually becoming a physician and his brother, the Rector of Wistanstow.

However, it was their younger sister, Ann, who would become the major player in this true Shropshire story. Temptress, murderess, manipulator, spoilt little girl? Certainly some of these descriptions apply, and some say all.

She was seven years old and motherless when her father died, leaving her to be brought up by her stepmother. She had been much loved by her father whose will stipulated that after the death of his third wife Elizabeth, the lease of the rectoral tithes should go to Ann. In addition she was also the beneficiary in the will of her maternal uncle and godfather, William Whitmore.

Robert Foulkes was born in 1634 at Mallwyd close to Montgomeryshire and Merioneth and was educated first at the Royal Free Grammar School, Shrewsbury and then at Oxford University where he matriculated in 1652. By the mid-1650s he was preaching in the villages in the Borders around Wales. He may even in those early days have preached in Stanton Lacy although there are no supporting records. What is known is that he had contact with the Atkinson home, for living in their household was Isabella Colbatch, whom he married at Ludlow parish church on 7 September 1657.

Isabella's father, a former Ludlow rector, had died when Isabella was only three years old and although records contradict each other about just when she came to live in the Atkinson household, it is clear that she had resided there for some time at the time of meeting Robert Foulkes and perhaps had helped Elizabeth with her three step-children. She would have known the young

Ann very well and would have been a very prominent fixture in her young life.

Some time after their wedding, Robert and Isabella moved into the Atkinson household. In 1660 King Charles II returned to the throne, Lord Craven returned to Shropshire from exile and Robert Foulkes was inducted as vicar at Stanton Lacy on 12 September 1660. The die was cast.

The first sign of unrest occurred in 1662 when the 12-year-old Ann accused Isabella of taking a diamond ring belonging to her, and Isabella in turn complained that Ann was becoming too familiar with her husband. Ann denied such a thing but later comments implied that by the time she was fifteen, she was very familiar indeed with Foulkes, and often in his company.

Further statements mentioned in the later court actions went further, stating that Ann would brazenly throw her arms around Foulkes' neck and kiss him in front of his wife and ask him if

The vicarage at Stanton Lacy, built on the site of Robert Foulkes' residence from 1660.

it made his wife jealous. On occasions she would suggest that if kissing her husband made Isabella jealous, she would give her greater cause for jealousy.

Perhaps Ann felt jealous of or abandoned by Isabella, who had brought this young man into their household and turned her attention to him. Unquestionably Ann had enjoyed a privileged upbringing, had been cosseted, protected and moved in affluent circles. Therefore an educated, polished charismatic young orator, used to swaying congregations and being the centre of attention, would be very much in-keeping with her aspirations.

For a time, however, life was settled, Foulkes appeared to enjoy the respect of the parishioners, his income was sufficient to live on and he was free with his advice and help to his flock. By 1674, Isabella had given birth to three children.

But signs of a storm were brewing.

The Hopton family were well-known in the village as a particularly disreputable clan and Reverend Robert Foulkes had denounced Richard Hopton from the pulpit as a dishonest man. His son William Hopton, the landlord of a local tavern with a reputation as a drunk, liar and fraud, cheated Elizabeth Atkinson out of leases that would eventually have gone to her stepdaughter Ann. The fraud was perpetrated with the help of Isabella Foulkes, presumably bitter about Ann's relationship with her husband. She forged Elizabeth's signature on letters to Lord Craven, transferring the leases from Ann's name into that of Elizabeth's niece, Mary Withers. As soon as the fraud was completed, Mary Withers left Elizabeth's household and married William Hopton.

During this time Ann Atkinson had been away from the village for about two years. The reason for her absence would become clearer later. When she discovered that she had been cheated out of her inheritance, she complained directly to Lord Craven, and the leases were reinstated in her name. William Hopton was enraged and threatened revenge on Ann. The Reverend Robert Foulkes was later to denounce Hopton as a drunkard, a liar, a swearer who sold ale on the Sabbath and who had a bastard child! Resentments simmered as Hopton plotted his revenge. Real stirrings of trouble appeared following a church service in the summer of 1676. Foulkes had preached a message to 'resist the devil' and as the parishioners were leaving the church, William Hopton was witnessed as pointing at Ann Atkinson who was leaving the church and heard to say, 'There the she-devil goes, let *him* resist *her*.'

Hopton had a powerful ally in Mary Withers who had been part of the Atkinson household and was privy to many of its secrets. She told him of the 1673 pregnancy, when Ann had been sent away to north Shropshire to her brother Francis' house. Francis was by then a curate at West Felton, and there she gave birth to a baby girl in May 1674. Afterwards Ann had returned briefly to Stanton Lacy before leaving once again for Bridgnorth and then London.

Mary had good cause to remember, for it was Elizabeth who had sent her to West Felton to collect Ann, and she recalled Ann being particularly weak and applying ointment on her breasts. She also told of Foulkes calling on Ann and staying for a couple of nights and witnessed Ann sewing what she believed to be child linen.

Furthermore Richard Hopton overheard a parishioner rebuking Reverend Robert Foulkes about the pregnancy and Isabella told him that she had learned of the pregnancy in letters between her husband and Ann and she knew that there was a financial settlement in which her husband had paid Ann's brother Francis, the curate, to assist in the baby's maintenance. It was also believed that Foulkes confessed to Isabella's brother John Colbatch, although Foulkes later denied any such confession. Given such information, it is less surprising that Isabella agreed to take part in the fraud to deny Ann the benefit of her inheritance. It was a way to get back at her.

Armed with all this information, William Hopton set out with Charles Pearce of Eastfields in the parish, determined to confirm the story and if possible track down the infant; he was hell-bent on the total destruction of the Reverend Robert Foulkes.

Their search revealed that a baby had indeed been born to Ann and baptised by Francis Atkinson, then was sent away to live with the Brey family in Llansantffraud, Montgomeryshire under the name of Mary Morris. They even discovered that there was a sum of five pounds to be paid annually towards the upkeep of the child.

Armed with all this damning information, Hopton was now determined to exact his revenge and finish Foulkes professionally. However he was aware that with his reputation and the likelihood of being accused of seeking vengeance, any accusation coming from him would be rejected. He elicited the help of Richard Chearme, churchwarden to Reverend Foulkes, who duly reported his vicar to the Bishop's court.

The bishop Doctor Herbert Croft was informed among other things that Reverend Robert Foulkes had been 'associating himself with and keeping company with Ann Atkinson at unseasonable times and in private places'. At a subsequent hearing in St Laurence's church, Ludlow, the bishop decreed that Foulkes was to avoid all contact with Ann Atkinson unless there were at least three or four other people of good repute present at the same time. Richard Chearme was unable to attend the second hearing because he allegedly had suffered an attack from the vicar!

For the time being at least, Foulkes had got away with it, but resentment, intrigue and violence was still simmering away in the Shropshire parish.

Foulkes, perhaps wounded by all the accusations, became quite cavalier in his behaviour in public. In front of a parishioner Martha Dovey, in Elizabeth's parlour, he told Ann as his wife Isabella passed by the window, 'See how my wife looketh with malice and envy. Jealousie will eat her up and I will keep her short enough and keep it all for thee.' Shockingly he appears to have had little shame or remorse for he talked again in front of

Martha Dovey telling Ann to tell Martha, 'what you have done with the little thing at West Felton' to which Ann responded, 'Tell it yourself for it concerns you as well as me.'

His heavy drinking and bawdiness became a talking point of the village. Eventually he lost all credibility, when one summer night in 1676, after a friendly word of advice from the Vicar of Bromfield warning him of the gossip and urging him to stay away from Ann which at the time he appeared to accept in good spirit, he decided to invite church-warden Richard Chearme and Francis Underwood for a drink at the vicarage. As the evening progressed he told them to go and fetch their wives and stay for dinner. Later that evening as the drink began to take its toll, he became aggressive and abusive and insulting to the men and sexually aggressive towards their wives.

As events got out of hand, Foulkes physically attacked Isabella. Her screaming frightened their maidservant who sent for the local constable. A large crowd, alerted by the commotion, gathered outside the vicarage. It was the Deputy Constable who responded and he immediately authorised William Hopton and Chearme to help him arrest Foulkes. Isabella was bleeding and crying upstairs and as Foulkes menaced them all, Hopton refused to go in but Chearme entered and was attacked with the fire tongs.

Eventually order was restored and once again Robert Foulkes was called into court to account for his behaviour – hardly the actions of a man of the church. The accusers were the usual anti-Foulkes brigade: the Hoptons, Chearme and Joseph Dovey. William Hopton testified that he had seen Foulkes at the alehouse of the widow Partridge, kissing and embracing her daughter who was known as a loose woman. It was mentioned that he was seen openly kissing and fondling Ann Atkinson and that there was talk of fornication and adultery between them and that there was talk of children or at least one child from their liaison.

Mary Withers and Martha Dovey both stated that they

had seen Foulkes in Ann's bedroom, fondling her. Chearme and his wife Margaret testified as to Foulkes and Ann's unashamed intimacy. Richard Chearme also recalled that when Foulkes told him that the Hoptons were rogues and knaves he had advised him to watch his words as they had friends connected with the Lord Bishop. Robert Foulkes allegedly responded, 'I care not a fart from my arse for the Lord Bishop, Chancellor nor any one of them.'

Further accusations insinuated that his wife Isabella was terrified of him and Hopton alleged that Foulkes had tried to stab her with his penknife and tried to strangle her. She had come to him for milk and other supplies fearing that her husband might try to poison her.

The list of accusations went on; that part of his income went to support his bastard child and it was alleged that he had denied Isabella the holy sacrament. In those days, church attendance was compulsory and non-attendance resulted in court appearances. It was particularly awkward with the Hoptons and Foulkes. Taking the sacrament from a priest for whom you had no respect was difficult and a priest should not allow anyone they considered to be in a state of sin to take communion unless they repented. The Hoptons refused to go to Reverend Foulkes' services but instead went to the nearby church at Culmington. Their defence was that they couldn't bear Foulkes's hypocrisy, believing that he was ungodly and unchaste; they had a case.

For many of the villagers, the Reverend Foulkes had lost not only credibility, but also his dignity and they were actively on the look-out to try and catch the vicar and Ann together. On one memorable occasion Hopton and Chearme arrived at Francis Underwood's house, who was a tenant of Ann Atkinson, in the belief that Foulkes was there with Ann.

Judith Underwood, in the absence of her husband, answered their knock and denied that Robert Foulkes was there. Nevertheless the men entered her house and checked all the rooms. Finding one door locked, they called out to Foulkes to remember what the Bishop had said. There was no response so they left the house and hid outside. Half an hour later Robert Foulkes emerged and the men called to him whether he has not 'ashamed to be there in company with a whore?' Foulkes continued to walk away as many of the villagers whistled, clapped and hooted their derision. William Hopton told the hearing that the couple met at that house on several other occasions.

The maidservant of the Foulkes household, Joan Wood, was sacked after he discovered that she had been visiting Hopton's house late at night, cavorting into the early hours. Possibly as an act of vengeance, she testified that Foulkes had propositioned her for sex. There were other more petty complaints, such as that he had neglected the youths of the village, had not visited the sick, had not turned up to church for services and had neglected several of his duties.

It was a long list, but a number of people came forward to defend him.

The Atkinson family denied knowledge of any affair between Foulkes and Ann. Yes, they had kissed from time to time, but only as a form of greeting, Ann had never been sexually active with any man. They had heard the rumour of a bastard child but it was totally without foundation and of course Foulkes and Isabella fell out from time to time, but generally they were happy and a well-balanced couple. Ann's brother Francis Atkinson, the rector at West Felton who had baptised the child, denied any knowledge of an affair or offspring! Clearly the Atkinson family had closed rank and were prepared to perjure themselves. Several of Foulkes's clerical friends also rallied to his support, as did a number of Stanton Lacy parishioners.

Reverend Robert Foulkes stated that his accusers had ganged up on him in a combined action, in order to keep their prosecution costs down. It was also in his favour that his main accuser William

Hopton was known to many as a fraudster, a cheat and a liar who would do anything for money, including the well-known case of attempting to defraud Ann Atkinson of her inheritance.

The village was seething with various lawsuits of neighbour against neighbour at the time, with people suing and counter-suing. Soon afterwards, William Hopton absconded with £1,000 of Lord Craven's money, for whom he was acting as an agent. William Hopton now disappears completely from the story and the case against Robert Foulkes is weakened. Then Francis Hutchinson, who had been inveigled as promoter of the action brought by his cousins, said he now wanted out. He said that of all the accusers, Richard Chearme was the most poisonous, consumed by hate and intent on vengeance. He was by now no longer a tenant of Elizabeth's, his position being totally compromised by events.

The case against Reverend Robert Foulkes looked to be falling apart and it looked as if he might get away with his unacceptable behaviour. However the accusing group's legal counsel, Richard Cornwall, knew the validity of the action and was aware of many of the facts and was determined to carry on.

The case had dragged on for many months and in February 1678 their enemies appeared to be in disarray. But any relief Ann and Foulkes might have felt was short-lived when a most remarkable twist occurred that turned the case upside down.

On 14 August 1678 one John Brabant was buried at St Laurence's church, Ludlow, and his son Somerset Brabant, now living in Worcestershire, attended the service to pay his last respects to his father and to comfort his mother. Following the funeral, that evening he visited several local taverns and, probably in a Ludlow tavern, he astounded the locals by telling them that he knew all about Foulkes and Ann, and had done so for four years.

His story had them riveted.

Four years earlier Somerset Brabant had been employed at the *Talbot Hotel* in Worcester and recalled that one night in September

1674 (when Ann was supposed to be miles away from Foulkes) she arrived at the hotel with a maidservant and some time later Robert Foulkes arrived and was given the room next-door to hers.

Whilst going about his hotel duties and visiting Foulkes' room, he saw him kissing and hugging Ann and noticed that the bed was 'very much tumbled'. Anticipating further action, Brabant later that night tiptoed up the stairs and into an adjoining room where he knew there was a hole in the wall. Putting his hand carefully into the hole he was able to pull away the fabric lining the wall. He witnessed them in the 'very act of uncleanness'.

After a short rest they repeated the process and later Brabant had to leave his spy-hole to supply them with food. After delivering their meal he returned to his vantage point and watched them once again endorse their feelings for each other in the most enthusiastic fashion. Brabant also recalled Ann begging Foulkes never to reveal what had happened between them and together they knelt by the hearth and made their mutual promise before Ann left his room to return to hers.

The following morning the maid told Somerset Brabant that Robert Foulkes had walked into Ann's room, put his hand under her bedclothes to grope her body and then turned his attentions to her maid, who immediately jumped out of the bed. Foulkes paid the bill for both rooms and they departed later that morning.

Obviously Somerset Brabant's evidence was that elusive first-hand evidence the prosecution had been longing for and would prove decisive, irrespective of the dubious quality of most of the accusers' hearsay.

Brabant did not appear to understand the value of his testimony and where it would lead, but any reluctance on his part to testify was over-ruled by the lawyers.

Events now moved quickly. On 20 August, Reverend Robert Foulkes was banned from preaching and on 6 September 1678 court proceedings started once again, this time focusing on Ann with the prosecution building a case against her. The facts presented concerned the illegitimate baby, her brazen flaunting of the affair, her indifference and cruelty towards Isabella, fresh evidence of her instigating amorous encounters with Foulkes citing letters she had written to her lover. It was obvious that the information had come from somebody within the Foulkes household, most probably Isabella. There was also fresh evidence that Foulkes had attempted to bribe witnesses.

While the prosecution were building their case, for Robert and Ann there was a final catastrophic event in their relationship. Ann discovered that she was once again pregnant. The couple left Stanton Lacy to be away from the very many prying eyes and went to London where they stayed in York Buildings off the Strand. What happened next is deduced from the pre-trial indictment.

It recorded that Ann Atkinson, a spinster, gave birth to a child on 12 December 1678 that was delivered in a private house without a midwife by Ann and her lover. It alleged that following the birth Robert Foulkes struck the child in the throat with a knife, causing a wound three inches long and half an inch wide from which the child died.

Leaving Ann behind to recover, Robert Foulkes left for Shropshire almost immediately but by the strangest quirk of fate, the baby's body was discovered. Foulkes was pursued and brought back to London. It is not known how the baby's body, which had been disposed of in the house's privy, was discovered: probably Ann's servant, realising the enormity of what had happened, raised the alarm.

The couple were both held in the notorious Newgate Prison renowned for filth, squalor and disease. As the trial approached, Ann started to distance herself from her erstwhile lover. Both pleaded not guilty. Ann claimed that during the birth she had been in severe pain and had wanted to send for help but Foulkes had refused, insisting that he would conduct the delivery.

Throughout the trial, Foulkes maintained his innocence, although he did confess privately to the Bishop of St Asaph, Dr William Lloyd, that after the birth, he had asked Ann what to do with the child and she had responded, 'Kill it' and had passed him the knife. He admitted throwing the dead baby into the privy office (toilet) and said Ann then got a curtain rail and pushed the tiny corpse further out of sight. The body may eventually have ended up in the Thames.

However Ann told the jury that after the birth Foulkes had taken the baby away, as she thought, to be taken care of by a nurse, and she denied any part in the murder. Ann, supported by her wealth and connections, was able to employ legal counsel and they blackened Foulkes character before a packed gallery who hung on every word during the trial. They suggested that Foulkes had been Ann's guardian and she had trusted him but he had betrayed and corrupted her from a very early age.

At the Lord Chief Justice's prompting, the jury took Ann's side and the Reverend Robert Foulkes was found guilty and sentenced to be hanged at Tyburn.

Following the trial, he was full of remorse and during a stay of execution he wrote a pamphlet, *An Alarme For Sinners*, to serve as a warning to others who might be tempted as he was. His confession was published at his request and became a national best-seller. However, he must have been devastated to be betrayed by the woman he had given up everything for, a soul-mate who deserted him in his hour of need. It was observed that Ann, immediately after the trial, entertained her lawyers in a nearby tavern, more relieved by her own good fortune than devastated at her lover's dismal fate.

On 31 January 1679, the Reverend Robert Foulkes, accompanied by several clergy, left by coach for Tyburn. He 'got onto the ladder', made an excellent speech before a large crowd, repenting of his sins and advising others to avoid his fate. He finished by saying,

'You may in me see what sin is, and what it will end in.' He was buried in the churchyard of St Giles in the Fields, Tyburn's parish.

What of Ann? She stayed in London for around three years waiting for the scandal to die down before returning to Stanton Lacy. However the Bishop Dr William Lloyd firmly believed that she was also guilty and vowed to take action, a view shared by Isabella. A communication was sent to the Archbishop of Canterbury stating 'this horrible woman appears to have escaped any form of punishment.' Sadly the records do not inform us of any action taken against Ann and after 1682 there is no further information as to her whereabouts.

This is a truly remarkable story and would do justice to any modern-day television drama, with all the many twists and turns and the range of Shropshire characters each with their own agenda. The true story is almost 400 years old, yet the frailty and vulnerability of man has not changed at all since those days.

What follows is the second of the two tales concerning two vicars of Shropshire: it could not be more different or more uplifting, this time demonstrating a priest's dedication, faith and willingness to make the ultimate sacrifice for a good cause.

Snow was falling, snow on snow, snow on snow, In the bleak midwinter long, long ago

The Shropshire hills in the spring, summer or autumn attract many walkers and hikers appreciative of the wild, unspoilt nature of much of the landscape.

The Long Mynd is a distinct feature, a high plateau about six miles long stretching from the village of Plowden to Ratlinghope and its barren moorland, dressed by heather and bilberry bushes, contains several steep valleys. In my research of this story I actually made the journey from Woolstaston to Ratlinghope on a beautiful, bright, hot sunny May day by car! I hasten to add that I did stop to walk down several of the little valleys and gulleys to try to get some idea of the remarkable journey made by the Reverend Carr.

I was overwhelmed by the unspoilt beauty of this wilderness and can very much appreciate the attraction for walkers and hikers attempting the trip from Woolstaston across the Long Mynd to Ratlinghope and perhaps on to Church Stretton. The descent by car to Church Stretton, however, down narrow, winding tracks with a sheer drop on one side wasn't altogether relaxing! I did however obtain a clear idea of what the journey must have entailed in the snow-battered winter of 1865 – a far different proposition from that of a bright sunny day.

The winter of 1865 was particularly severe and went down on record as having the heaviest fall of snow for 51 years. It was particularly severe on the local populace of the Stretton Hills: water supplies were frozen over, fuel was hard to come by and the snow made travelling extremely difficult.

As January 1866 progressed there was no respite: the snow continued to fall and massive snow-drifts blocked roads making movement impossible as winds banked the snow up against houses already frozen over from severe frost. Anything that could be burnt was used as fuel, to try to bring some suggestion of warmth to houses with no central heating, no double-glazing and none of the comforts we now take for granted. Strong icy winds cut through what little protective clothing was available.

The Reverend Edmund Donald Carr, the Rector of St Michael's in the small village of Woolstaston just east of the Long Mynd, was undeterred. He had a job to do and he was going to do it.

He set out from his rectory on Sunday 29 January and although the route was barely discernable, buried under impacted snow and ice, he battled his way through to the local church. For a moment he sheltered by the church door to catch his breath, brush off the snow and to greet the organist and the small choir who had also dutifully made it to the church. Inside the church it was still very cold but the bell ringers got to work and the organist climbed into his loft and instructed the boys to start pumping the organ.

The villagers heard the comforting sounds of normality and, wrapped in whatever layers of clothing they had, they arrived at the church clutching their bibles and each in turn was greeted with a handshake by the smiling Reverend Carr.

Inside the church, the warden had by now managed to light a wood stove and lighted candles scattered around the church gave an illusion of heat and a modicum of warmth. The singing and the sound of the organ carried outside to a silent, beautiful white landscape, marred only by footprints. Very soon the congregation hurried away back home but the Reverend Carr anxiously scanned the horizon as he said goodbye to his flock. For him the day was far from over and he was searching for some sign of improvement in the weather.

At that time, as today, Rectors were responsible for more than one parish and Carr also had responsibility for a Shropshire parish in the hill-mining district of Stiperstones. The church, St Margaret's, was in the village of Ratlinghope and the parish of around 300 people was too small to sustain their own curate, so for eight years

Reverend Carr had been visiting each sabbath and had never missed a service. He was extremely conscientious and proud of his record and despite the weather, he had no intention of letting his flock down. For the last eight years, accompanied by his manservant, he had travelled along the northern end of the Long Mynd to Ratling-hope and knew the area like the back of his hand.

Despite warnings from the church wardens and his family not to go, as the conditions were dangerous, Carr decided to miss his lunch and make an earlier start in his battle against the snow-drifts.

As he set off with his manservant and horses, little did he suspect what he was in for. They had barely travelled half a mile outside Woolstaston, up the steep incline out of the village, when it became obvious that the horses could not cope with the depth of the snow and the decision was taken for the servant to return with the horses and for Carr to battle on alone.

In his book, *A Night in the Snow*, written after his ordeal, he recalled: 'The journey proved more difficult than I had ever imagined... I could only get through on my hands and knees.'

Nevertheless, this remarkable man battled through to Ratling-hope, a little late but much appreciated by the astounded congrega-

Woolstaston: the start of Reverend Carr's remarkable journey.

111

tion. It was said that when he arrived he was cheerful but very, very cold and knowing that he had to get back home he got through the service quite quickly and then enjoyed a little refreshment with the churchwarden before embarking on the return journey.

The weather conditions worsened as the Reverend Carr left Ratlinghope for Woolstaston. No sooner had he reached the outskirts of the village than he was stopped in his tracks by a gale force wind whipping up the snow. He had difficulty in standing and was thrown to the ground on several occasions and had to turn his battered face away from the wind in order to breathe.

The first half-mile leading out of the village is up a very steep incline and must have exhausted him almost immediately. Nevertheless, he battled on.

He knew that he was crossing wild moorland in the right direction when he was able to identify Wild Moor pool. Soon, he thought, he would be home to the comfort of his family and fireside.

His optimism was short-lived. Visibility reduced to just feet and as he stumbled along, night was falling and he realised that he was lost. Confused, battered by the wind and snow, he stumbled around and then fell headlong down a ravine in a small valley.

He later recalled that the valley bottom was covered by snow to a depth that made walking through it virtually impossible. It was later noted that some of the snow-drifts in the valley had reached depths of twenty feet. Ravines, small valleys and gulleys were all covered up, as were all recognisable features. Stepping into what one hoped was firm ground could mean a fall into snow many feet thick.

Reverend Carr's entire body was by now covered in snow. His woollen and cloth garments were not only wet but frozen solid and barely protective. His face was taking on the appearance of a snow monster. Whiskers were covered in ice, mini-icicles formed around his eyebrows and his hair was stiff with frozen snow. Although he had a brandy flask with him, he recalled that his hands were so numb that he could not lift it to his lips.

A photograph of the Long Mynd clearly illustrates one of the many gulleys that would have become invisible in the heavy snow.

The effect of falling into the ravine and the icy whipping wind had left balls of ice in the crooks of his elbows and knees. It was dark and as he tried to settle down for the night, he later admitted that at that point he almost gave up the struggle for survival.

Somehow he got through that night and the dawn greeted him with freezing fog. Still lost, he continued to wander around, not knowing where he was. Time and again he slipped and rolled down slopes before realising that he was partially snow blind. He kept getting back on his feet and continued to walk. Eventually he came to a small stream which he recognised as Light Spout waterfall, but his joy was short-lived when somehow he lost his boots. However, he recalled that losing his boots had made little difference to him, as his feet were so cold already.

When he came to an area he recognised as Carding Mill Valley, he was overjoyed to hear the voices of children playing in the snow.

He called out to the children whom he could barely see but to no avail – no one responded. He later realised that the children had seen him but he was such a terrifying sight that they were too frightened to approach him: he was protruding out of a snowdrift with just his head in view, covered in ice with a beard sporting icicles and eyes unable to focus. It must have been a terrifying sight for any young child.

Eventually a brave little girl ventured towards him and after gazing at him for some time said, 'You look just like Mr Carr of Woolstaston.'

He had made it.

He was brought to a nearby cottage and served hot tea but was unable to eat the food kindly provided to him. After resting and borrowing hat, boots and stockings, he set off for Church Stretton, about a mile away and arrived at the *Crown Hotel* at about 2pm.

From the time of leaving Ratlinghope, Reverend Carr had been out in the wild, alone for 22 hours. News of his survival spread rapidly through the valley and his manservant forced a horse and cart through the snow to Church Stretton to bring him home. The village of Woolstaston and the vicar's family, who must have given up all hope of his survival, were overjoyed.

After gathering his senses he discovered that, despite his prolonged exposure, frostbite and gangrene had not manifested themselves. Reverend Carr later wrote a book about his ordeal which raised funds for the church restoration.

Another very positive result came with the decision to build a rectory in Ratlinghope to ensure that clergymen would not have to travel difficult or long journeys when servicing several parishes.

Shropshire's Reverend Edmund Donald Carr was the total opposite to Reverend Robert Foulkes. He was dedicated to his faith; he was a happily married man with a family and would not be distracted from his duty even when his life was very much in peril. He commanded respect from his parishioners, even more so after surviving his ordeal. Many must have felt that God was indeed on the side of their vicar and had worked a miracle in saving him.

The tiny Shropshire hill village of Ratlinghope has two more strings to its bow. It was the village featured in a TV episode of *Dalziel and Pascoe* and in 2005 it was the main location for the BBC sitcom, *Green, Green Grass.*

An interesting footnote (no pun intended): the boots worn by Reverend Carr on his epic journey were found and are today preserved in the Shrewsbury Museum.

St Margaret's Church at Ratlinghope was granted its own rectory following Reverend Carr's incredible survival.

Chapter Five

BIRTHPLACE OF CHAMPIONS

For its size, Shropshire has produced an inordinate number of sportsmen who have not only been champions in their own field but who have become legends in the sporting history of Great Britain and whose deeds have earned them worldwide acclaim.

One such man was Captain Matthew Webb who, in the 19th century, became world-renowned for his swimming exploits. Britain's two greatest sportsmen of the 1940s and 1950s, jockey Sir Gordon Richards and footballer Billy Wright dominated the headlines, and in the 1980s and 1990s two of golf's greatest players on the world scene, and still competing today, are Salopians Sandy Lyle and Ian Woosnam. Shropshire is also the home of former World Boxing Champion Richie Woodhall, now a respected boxing commentator, and professional boxing trainer to the British Olympic boxing squad for 2012.

The first celebration in this chapter is of a Shropshire man who was not a sports champion but who was a champion of sports. The biggest sporting event on the planet is the Olympic Games, a truly global event every four years. Few people outside Much Wenlock are aware that the inspiration came from their tiny village.

William Penny Brookes 1809-1895

The inspiration and founder of the modern International Olympic Games, William Penny Brookes, was born in Much Wenlock in 1809. He came from an affluent family and followed his doctor father into the medical profession after studying in London, Paris and Italy. After qualifying he returned to Much Wenlock in 1831 and took over his late father's practice, living in the family's large town house in Wilmore Street.

His sense of community was perhaps sharpened by his privileged circumstances and he became a Justice of the Peace, a Commissioner for Roads and Taxes and he took an active interest in matters concerning the county, particularly the renovation of some of its historic buildings.

In 1841 he established the Wenlock Agricultural Reading Society which became a lending library for those seeking information and ideas. The concept of shared ideals caught on, and other Much Wenlock societies sprang up focusing on subjects such as art and botany.

As a doctor he believed in the benefits of exercise for health and well-being, so in 1850 he formed the Wenlock Olympian Class. Its aim was to 'promote the moral, physical and intellectual improvement of the inhabitants' by holding an annual Games, and as Brookes insisted, it was open to 'every grade of man'.

The very first of the 'Games' was held that year, opening with a procession in which the competitors marched ahead of the spectators through the decorated streets, led by a band, to the 'stadium' on Much Wenlock Racecourse. In 1858 the Games moved to Windmill Meadow, later renamed the Linden Field, and today called the Gaskell Recreation Grounds, still the main site of the annual Wenlock Games.

The Games were intended to have a competitive element but

were also designed for the entertainment of the watching crowds. There were three elements: ancient Greek-styled athletics; English sports such as football and cricket; and fun competitions such as blindfold wheelbarrow racing and a catch-a-piglet contest.

From its inception, and over the ensuing years, the Wenlock Games became ever more popular and diverse, with competitors travelling from as far afield as London and Liverpool in order to compete and win the coveted silver cups and medals. Further developments led to the formation by Brookes of the Shropshire Olympian Games in 1861 and a new concept was introduced: the Games were hosted and financed by a different town each year.

The concept continued to grow and in 1866 the National Olympian Association was set up by Brookes and his committee, encompassing Athletics, Gymnastics, Boating, Swimming and other sports. The resultant first three-day Festival of games was held at Crystal Palace, London. The event was a massive success attended by an estimated 10,000 spectators and competitors, and it is recorded that a young man, W.G. Grace, who would later make his name in a different field, won the 440-yard hurdle race!

Naturally such a success caused other spin-off organisation to blossom and the Amateur Athletic Club was formed for 'amateurs and gentlemen only' from public schools and the Oxbridge set. This was a direct contradiction of Brookes' principle of being 'open to every grade of man' but as it evolved into the Amateur Athletic Association (the AAA) and became the UK's governing sports body, it was forced to change its stance.

Meanwhile the Athens Olympian Games was launched in 1859 and Brookes sent a prize on behalf of the Wenlock Olympian Committee. The winner Petros Velissarios became the first Honorary Member of the Wenlock Olympian Society.

Brookes was conscious of the Greek roots of the Olympic Games and was keen to revive their interest on a broader level than just Athens. In 1877, following his request, he received a silver cup from the King of Greece to be presented at the National Olympian Games, held that year in Shrewsbury. Brookes' efforts to stimulate international interest in the Olympics led to a lifelong friendship with the Greek Chargé d'Affaires in London, as he continued to encourage the Greek government to revive the Ancient Games in all their glory – but to make them open to international competitors.

William Brookes persistently petitioned Parliament to have sport and exercise made compulsory in all schools and he campaigned actively in this direction for over 30 years.

A man of similar interests to Brookes, Baron De Coubertin, who was the organiser of the International Congress of Physical Education, visited England in 1889 to learn how England approached sports education in schools. Brookes learned of his visit and invited him to come the following year to the Wenlock Olympian Games.

So in 1890, Coubertin came to Much Wenlock and stayed as a guest with the Brookes' family and, despite their age difference, (Brookes 82 and Coubertin 27), their ideas and ideals were the same. Brookes confided in the young Frenchman his dream to revive the Olympic Games in Athens on an international scale. At the post-Wenlock Games dinner held at *The Raven Inn*, Coubertin gave an address to 60 guests, in which he gave his support; and on his return to France, he expressed delight in having found fellow enthusiasts, interested in sport for all.

William Penny Brookes died in December 1895 but not before learning that the Board of Education had agreed to include physical education as part of the curriculum in all schools. Sadly he did not live to see fulfilled his other life-long ambition: an Olympic Games revived on an international basis. This finally took place in April 1896, just four months after his death.

In his obituary, Baron Coubertin stated that Brookes was responsible for the revival of the modern International Olympic Games.

In 1994 the President of the International Olympic Games, Juan Antonio Samaranch, visited the Brookes' family grave in the grounds of the Holy Trinity Church, Much Wenlock, just a stone's throw from the family home on Wilmore Street. After laying a wreath, the President told the world's press, 'I came to pay tribute and homage to Dr Brookes who really was the founder of the Modern Olympic Games.'

The Games at Much Wenlock continue to be held over every second weekend of July every year and now also include bowls, archery, clay pigeon shooting, fencing, golf, tennis and volleyball. There have been some memorable moments, but perhaps the one that would have given William Brookes most pleasure featured Alison Williamson gaining a Bronze Medal for archery at the 2004 International Olympics in Athens. Alison had won a silver medal at the 1981 Wenlock Games as a ten-year-old, and her development into an international athlete from a Wenlock Olympian is a testament to Brookes' original concept.

The starting point of the Olympian trail is at the Much Wenlock Museum on the High Street.
The walk is approximately 1.3 miles.

Much Wenlock is quite rightly proud of its connection to the Olympic Games and the town has an Olympian Trail, which is a series of bronze plaques set in the pavements starting and finishing at the museum and directing visitors around the sites and buildings linked to the Wenlock Olympian movement.

Captain Matthew Webb 1848-1883

Every schoolboy once knew the answer to the question: 'Who was the first man to swim the English Channel?' The answer: 'Captain Webb!'

The Industrial Revolution was in full swing when Matthew Webb was born in Dawley on 19 January 1848 to Matthew and Sarah, the second-born of their eight children. His father was a surgeon and the family enjoyed a comfortable standard of living and were respected in their locality.

The young Matthew learned to swim in the strong currents of the River Severn and actually saved a younger brother from drowning in the river close to Ironbridge in 1863. From a very early age Matthew had an affinity with the sea and when he was twelve years old he was set on a maritime career and went to Liverpool where he joined the Conway training ship.

His career at sea flourished and he travelled the world during which time he discovered that he had a natural aptitude for swimming. It is believed that on one occasion while his ship was mid-Atlantic, a colleague fell overboard and Webb dived in after him. His attempt at a rescue failed but he was given a not-insignificant sum of £100 for his attempt.

He reached the zenith of his maritime career when he became a very young master with the Cunard Line but eventually quit his job as Captain of the steamship, *Emerald*. In 1874, at the age of 26, it was his intention to become a professional swimmer and in particular to concentrate on long-distance, endurance swimming. It was a brave decision and he took an even bolder step when he resolved to swim the English Channel, a feat never accomplished before. But it was also a shrewd decision because of the impact and the publicity that even a failed attempt would bring.

His first attempt in mid-August 1875 ended in failure after seven hours, and when he resolved to try once again, he was under no illusion as to what was before him. Smearing his body with porpoise oil to protect against the cold, he again entered the water close to the Admiralty Pier, Dover, on 24 August 1875.

The swim was long and extremely difficult. As he neared Calais, the passengers and crew of *The Maid of Kent* who were observing his final stage, all gathered on the rails of the ship and started to sing loudly *Rule Britannia*. Webb wrote in his diary that this inspired him through the final stage and he finally made it. Captain Matthew Webb of Shropshire therefore became the first man to swim the English Channel and would forever be commemorated in the set questions of countless quiz-masters!

The news spread like wildfire and when he arrived back in Shropshire, huge cheering crowds greeted him at Wellington railway station and accompanied him all the way back to Dawley where he was welcomed by a brass band in a fitting tribute to their conquering hero.

He became a national figure and his reputation spread around the world because, for its time, a swim across open sea-water such as the English Channel was dangerous. Just over 19 nautical miles involved Webb swimming for 21 hours and 45 minutes against strong currents, wind and amongst heavy cross-channel shipping, with his only protection porpoise oil, spread over his exposed skin. Although the time of his crossing is quite specific, one record claims that, due to the tide, he was unable to land and spent several hours being swept up and down the coastline before stepping ashore after 39 hours!

The London Stock Exchange set up a testimonial fund for him that raised £2,424. After giving his father £500, he invested the rest to provide himself with income later in his life.

In order to capitalise on his new-found fame, he moved to London and took up residence at 21 Tavistock Crescent, Kensington. His parents sadly did not live long enough to enjoy the fruits of their son's fame and by 1877, within two years of the triumph, both had passed away. Webb continued his swimming training and was in demand overseas on a series of lecture tours. By 1880 he had met and married 21-year-old Madeline Kate Chaddock and they went on to have two children, Matthew and Mary.

For a time Webb flourished in his profession and, in addition to his lectures, he took part in financially rewarding races in America, just off Manhattan, and defeated the American champion Paul Boyton in a race off Nantasket that was billed as the World Championship. In an amazing display of endurance, he floated in a tank of water at the Boston Horticultural Show for 128 hours, winning £1,000 for the feat.

However, on 24 July 1883 Webb accepted a challenge too far. Whether it was for the money – £12,000, a huge sum – or the fame, he undertook what no one had survived. He attempted to swim under and across the Niagara Falls!

he was about to attempt. A friend Robert Watson, a witness to what occurred, recalled, 'As we stood face to face, I compared the fine handsome sailor I had first met with the broken-spirited and terribly altered appearance of the man who now courted death in the whirlpool rapids. His object was not suicide but money and imperishable fame.'

His description of Webb at the time does not give the impression of a fit, trained athlete determined to succeed! Webb himself is alleged to have said, 'If I die they will do something for my wife.'

Although his wife is purported to have been unaware of his attempt, nevertheless there was huge publicity and thousands attended the event, many brought in by special trains.

As the huge crowds lined both banks of the river, Webb dived in and some reports indicate that he hit his head on a rock just beneath the surface, but other reports say that he was swimming strongly against a whirlpool when suddenly he was taken by a current, threw his arms up in the air and disappeared under the water. It was the death of a hero!

There is a 1909 monument to him in his hometown, Dawley, Shropshire, which bears the inscription, 'Nothing great is easy.'

When I visited the town in June 2009, the statue, which had been standing in the centre of the main street, had been removed for repairs; nevertheless there is a street named after him in Dawley and an office building.

Captain Matthew Webb was a local Shropshire hero, a national champion and an athlete of international acclaim.

Sir Gordon Richards 1904-1986

Very rarely is one man so talented that he has been able to dominate his sport in the way Gordon Richards dominated horse racing, the 'Sport of Kings', from his first win of a major classic, the Oaks, in 1930 to his retirement from the sport following an injury in 1954, ending a career in which he achieved 4,870 wins!

He was born the son of a miner on 5 May 1904 into a large family at Ivy Row in the small Shropshire village of Donnington Wood, later part of the new town of Telford. Shortly afterwards, the family moved to a four-acre site at Wrockwardine Wood, Plow Road, Telford and shrewdly built three houses on the plot, living in one and renting out the others.

From birth Gordon was influenced by horses as his father

bred and reared pit ponies at their home. He was riding bareback as a toddler and from around the age of seven he was taking his share of driving the family pony and trap passenger service between the villages of Wrockwardine Wood and Oakengates to the station.

He was small and often had to stand up and lengthen the reins in order to control the ponies – and this would be the style that he adopted in racing in all the major Classics in the years to come. He often commented that he had never had a riding lesson and that his style was totally natural and had evolved from those early days driving the pony and trap standing up.

He left school at the age of 13 and started work as a junior clerk in the St George's branch of the Lilleshall Company engineering works. He rode to work on a pony, leaving it tethered in a field ready for the return trip. Clerical work was a drudge and he unsuccess-fully applied several times for jobs as a stable boy. Eventually his persistence paid off and he became stable boy to Jimmy White who owned the Foxhill Stable at Wanborough in Wiltshire, where he worked for trainer Martin Hartigan.

It was a big wrench leaving his large, happy Shropshire family but his ambition was fuelled and the opportunity was there to be taken. He was good at his job and totally at one with the horses but was still searching for that elusive break. It came during a friendly soccer match between neighbouring stables. The match was drawn 3-3 with five minutes left when Foxhill stables were granted a penalty and owner Jimmy White promised Richards that, if he took the penalty and scored, he would reward him with a ride at Lincoln the following day; such stories are the stuff of legends. He scored, he rode at Lincoln and the pages of history started to turn.

Shortly afterwards he won his first-ever race at Leicester in March 1921 and in 1925 achieved his dream of becoming a full-time professional jockey with Captain Tommy Hogg at Russley Park. In that first year he astounded the racing fraternity by winning 118 races, earning himself the title Champion Jockey of Great Britain.

Nobody imagined he would go on to win that title a record 26 times in the ensuing years!

To the purist, this young man was a phenomenon who defied the accepted methods of riding. He rode virtually upright with a slightly twisted torso and long reins, and no amount of experience would ever change that winning style.

His early triumph however was short-lived as he contracted tuberculosis and spent many months recuperating in a sanatorium in Norfolk, missing the entire 1926 racing season.

In 1927, he was back in the saddle and back to winning ways, regaining the Champion Jockey title. In 1928, he accepted a retainer from Frederick Darling at Beckhampton and that year won the Ebor Handicap. However his best years, unbelievably, were still to come, despite his racing weight around this time being under 7 stones. The great races started to fall to him. In 1930 he won the Oaks and the St Leger and in 1932, when winning 259 races in one season, he broke the record that had stood for 50 years. The racing world knew that they were privileged to be witnessing the greatest jockey that the sport had ever seen.

In wartime Britain, he cheered up the jaded populace with his deeds and in 1942 he won four of the five Classics: the Oaks, the 2000 Guineas, the St Leger and the 1000 Guineas. The only major Classic to evade him that year was the Derby.

The years rolled by and his successes continued, this time under Noel Murless at Newmarket, who had taken over Darling's stable following his retirement.

As 1953 approached, Gordon Richards had won 14 of the Classics, but he still could not win that elusive one, the Derby. It was amazingly similar to another legendary sporting figure in a similar scenario: Sir Stanley Matthews had won every honour that football had to offer, except the FA Cup. As 1953 progressed these two great sportsmen, now nearing retirement, were both striving for that elusive final win.

1953 was a momentous year in many ways: young Queen Elizabeth II ascended the throne, Hillary and Tenzing conquered Everest, England regained the cricket Ashes from Australia and Stan Matthews received his much-deserved FA Cup winners' medal at the age of 38, old for a footballer.

For Gordon Richards the year was equally momentous. Just days before the race he was knighted for his services to British horse-racing, the first and only jockey to date to receive such an honour. However, he was 49 years old, and many watching racing fans realised that, as he lined up on Pinza at the Derby his 28th attempt, this could be his last chance to win the one big race that had always eluded him. He was in second place for much of the race but, nearing the finish and using his skill and great timing, he judged the sprint for the line correctly and hit the front to overtake the Queen's horse and fulfil his life's dream. The watching spectators at Epsom, estimated at half a million, erupted into a frenzy, as did the millions watching on television or listening to the radio. The Queen, despite her own disappointment, called him from the winner's enclosure to personally congratulate him.

The following year, 1954, Sir Gordon suffered a pelvic injury and was forced to retire from active racing but joined the ranks as a trainer, adviser and racing manager to Lady Beaverbrook and Sir Michael Sobell.

Although such a small man, he was a sporting giant. Despite all the adulation, the honours and the successes, he was popular with all who had the good fortune to know him. He remained humble, kind and well-mannered, a tribute to the close-loving family that gave him such support.

His wife Margery pre-deceased him in 1982 and when he died in 1986, he left behind a son and a daughter.

In Shropshire there was a pub named after his exploits, *Champion Jockey*, in Donnington and at the Oakengates Theatre there is a Pinza suite named after his memorable Derby-winning horse.

Billy Wright 1924-1994

While Salopians were basking in the pride of local lad Sir Gordon Richards who was dominating the headlines in the racing world, yet another Shropshire hero was making headlines in his own genre, William Ambrose (Billy) Wright, Captain of England and Wolves soccer supremo.

When in July 1958, as the most renowned soccer player in the country, he married Joy Beverley of the hugely popular singing group the Beverley Sisters, the press attention and the public interest reached a level never known before. The couple were the 'Beckhams' of their day. Billy Wright was one of the very first football players to command such attention, and he was in demand for television celebrity appearances and advertisements. He was even hounded by the press.

As a player he was tough but throughout a career embracing over 500 games in the gold and black of Wolverhampton Wanderers and 105 appearances for England, he was never punished for foul play, never booked by the referee and never dismissed from the pitch; a remarkable achievement. He was well-mannered, modest and polite despite attention from all quarters which was on occasion invasive and unwelcome.

Born in Ironbridge on 6 February 1924, he had soccer in his blood: father Tommy, an iron foundry worker, was a useful footballer who supported Aston Villa and his mother was an ardent West Bromwich Albion supporter. Young Billy grew up supporting Arsenal.

Billy was short, stocky and fair, just like his father, and as a 12-year-old attending Madeley Senior School, despite his size, they played him at centre forward and in one memorable game he scored ten goals in a 12-0 win!

He recalls that the first big match he ever saw was in 1936

128

when his beloved Arsenal played Wolverhampton: little did he know that his life would later be devoted to the Wolves.

He played in the local leagues and one day Wolves spotted his potential and he joined their ground staff at a wage of £2 per week. It meant moving into lodgings in the Wolverhampton area and spending his days training, scrubbing baths, cleaning boots, sweeping terraces and any odd jobs that needed doing around the Molineux ground. Three nights per week were spent attending Technical School where he studied metal engineering, for in those days all professional footballers were advised to have a second career to fall back on as their playing time was short and prone to injury.

Just as his career was starting, the Second World War broke out and in 1942, at the age of 18, he was called up. The very first highlight of his career was an appearance in a losing League War Cup semi-final playing for Wolves against West Brom in May

Billy Wright in action, illustrated by Ross, in Charles Buchan's Football Monthly, April 1952.

1942. Just weeks later he broke an ankle and feared that his career was over just as it was starting – but he quickly recovered and featured in several games for the British Army.

When the war ended in 1945 he resumed his footballing career and in 1946/7 he not only became a full-time professional footballer but also captain of Wolverhampton Wanderers.

It was the start of a relationship that was to prove immensely successful and Wolves won the FA Cup at Wembley in 1948/49 against Leicester City in front of a 100,000-crowd and won the much-coveted Football League Championship in 1953/4 and again in 1957/8 and 1958/9. It was also during the 1950s that Wolves broke new ground when they invited Spartak Moscow to play at Molineux in 1954 and also the world-famous Hungarian team, Honved, in great international matches under floodlights, attended by gates of 55,000 and televised to huge audiences. These games sparked great interest and they were the start of the now immensely popular European Championships.

Wright's time with Wolves was arguably the most successful era in that famous club's history but he was also building a career on the international scene. He received his first cap for England against Northern Ireland on 28 September 1946 playing at right half, and two years later to the day he was captaining England once again against Northern Ireland. It was an incredible honour because the England team at that time included such legends of the game as Stanley Matthews, Stan Mortensen, Tom Finney and Frank Swift and to become leader of such men spoke volumes for Wright's qualities.

Wright went on to make 105 appearances for England, a record that stood for many years and has only been surpassed by Bobby Moore, Sir Bobby Charlton, Peter Shilton and recently by David Beckham. However his 90 appearances as captain of England is a record that still stands today.

He played for his country in two World Cup series, 1954

in Switzerland and 1958 in Sweden and in addition he was voted Footballer of the Year in 1952. After receiving his 100th cap against Scotland in 1959 he was given a Civic Banquet at the Wolverhampton Town Hall attended by 700 guests. Later when touring Brazil he was given a gold medal from the Brazilian FA to commemorate his landmark achievement and then also in 1959 he was awarded the CBE for his services to British football. He attended Buckingham Palace in November 1959 with his wife Joy and his very proud father Tommy to receive his award from the Queen.

He took the decision to retire as a Wolves player in 1959 after 21 years service to the club, the only club that he was ever interested in playing for. *The Times* newspaper described him as a 'National Treasure', an indication of the respect that he had commanded over the years.

He became the recipient of an honour afforded to very few when he was the subject of the TV programme, *This Is Your Life* in 1961. When the Football Association made him a Life Member he became the first professional player to receive such an honour and this was followed in 2002 when Billy Wright became the first player to be inducted into the National Football Museum's Hall of Fame.

Although blessed by considerable success, Billy Wright would have said that his greatest achievement was his marriage to the singer Joy Beverley.

They met by chance in April 1958 when Billy offered to show Joy's son, from her first marriage, his medals and trophies, to while away the time while Joy was topping the bill in Wolverhampton. However the fates decreed that the date was changed and Joy came to see the medals too. Soon the couple, despite their busy schedules, while Billy was in Sweden for the World Cup, were finding time to write and to telephone each other. By now the press were closing in and when Billy returned from Sweden, Joy met him at the airport surrounded by hordes of newsmen and photographers shouting, 'When are you getting married?'

They fixed a date for the marriage but kept it an absolute secret and when they set off on in July 1958 for the Poole Registry Office they had no idea of the reception awaiting them: there were thousands of members of the public and press.

On 5 April 1959 Joy gave birth to the couple's daughter, Victoria Ann. Joy came from a close, loving family and for her and Billy to have their own family unit helped ease the pressures on their 'goldfish bowl existence'.

After retiring from playing, Billy Wright worked as a football coach at several clubs before finally taking the big step of managing Arsenal in 1962, the club that he had followed as a small boy before his Wolverhampton days. Like many before and after him, he discovered that just because you were a great player it does not necessarily follow that you will become a great manager and in 1966 his contract at Arsenal was terminated.

Soon he found himself another role in the great game, becoming Head of Sport for Central TV, the forerunner of many similar programmes such as *Match of the Day*.

In his final years, with Billy's health failing, Sir Jack Hayward co-opted him onto the board of Wolverhampton Wanderers, stating that his experience and expertise would be of great value. Part of the great Molineux Stadium was named the Billy Wright Stand.

Billy Wright CBE, once known as the Ironbridge Rocket, died on 3 September 1994 aged 70. This Shropshire man was unquestionably one of England's greatest-ever soccer players.

Sandy Lyle 1958-

I suspect not too many people know that one of the finest golfers ever produced by these islands and indeed at one time rated by many as the greatest golfer in the world, actually comes from Shropshire. Most people believe that Sandy Lyle, because of his Scottish parents and ancestry, and pride in representing Scotland over the years, must have been born in Scotland. But he was not only born in Shropshire, but was brought up in the county and here developed his love, expertise and ability for the great game of golf.

His parents, Alex and Agnes Lyle, worked on their pig farm at Milngavie near Glasgow and eventually gave up the struggle, converting the land into the Glober Golf Course. Sandy's father was himself a fine golfer and had played in the 1953 British Open. The family relationship with Shropshire began in 1955 when Alex Lyle accepted the job as club professional at Hawkstone Park, midway between Shrewsbury and Whitchurch.

Hawkstone Park was the ancestral home of the Hills, one of Shropshire's most powerful families. During the 17th century the Hill family started to develop the park into a fantastic spectacle. Its 15 miles of paths are studded with caves, a grotto, secret tunnels and a medieval Red Castle; several follies were added, including a White Tower, and caves with an Arthurian theme were embellished with exotic statues. It became such an unusual and enjoyable place that from the early 1800s, it was opened to the public and remains open to this day.

Today Hawkstone, although it retains its magnificent grounds housing two superb golf courses, is a very different place to that entrusted to the Lyle family in 1955. The hotel today is larger and more extensive than the original and the new clubhouse is a superb facility with its golf shop, restaurant, meeting rooms and balcony with panoramic views over the scenic golf course with its magnificent cliffs and the Follies over-looking the fairways. Its most famous son Sandy Lyle is remembered in the clubhouse with his portrait, a wall plaque recording his triumphs, a framed autographed Ryder Cup celebration dinner menu signed by all the participants and a Sandy Lyle trophy competed for annually.

Hawkstone is a superb complex boasting two championship courses and a luxury hotel set in 400 acres of beautiful country. However, when the Lyles arrived with their two daughters, it was far from luxurious. The family found it isolated, in the middle of nowhere, and their house was tiny and infested with vermin. It was a nightmare for a young mother with children but things had improved a little when on 9 February 1958 Alexander Walter Barr Lyle was born to them in Shropshire. The owners of Hawkstone decided to put the whole property on the market and Alex Lyle borrowed money from the bank and with a consortium of local businessmen, they bought the house, the grounds and the hotel for £60,000. At the time it was seen as a brave move but has proven to be extremely lucrative.

The family worked hard, Alex being the golf professional gave lessons and performed odd jobs, his wife with the baby Sandy in his pram parked outside her kitchen overlooking the 18th tee, did the bookkeeping, cooking and housework.

Sandy wrote in his autobiography, *To The Fairway Born*, that he had an idyllic, almost blissful upbringing in Shropshire. Surrounded by golf, he had his own miniature set of clubs and his own trolley and there was a report and a photograph of him when he was just under four stating that he could drive a golf ball 80 yards. At the age of eight it is recorded that he completed a round of 18 holes of golf in 127 strokes, an amazing indication of what was to come. At the age of 11 he won the August Medal at Hawkstone, with 85 a net 64, winning for himself a silver teaspoon, the first of countless trophies and perhaps earning the ire of the members of Hawkstone golf club at being beaten by an 11-year-old!

The Hawkstone golf course is overlooked by one of the Follies built by the Hill family; the Gothic Arch on top of Grotto Hill.

However, Sandy's father made sure that his feet were kept firmly on the ground and that he remained unassuming at all times. Although he virtually had access to practice facilities all the time, his father ensured that he did not become a nuisance.

Hawkstone for a young lad was a fabulous place with its rivers, ravines, caves, boating on the lake, fishing in the waters, bike riding through the woods and sledging down the hills in the winter snow, as well as offering the chance to practice golf whenever required. It was truly a privileged upbringing and gave him a tremendous platform on which to build for the rest of his life.

In 1972, he became the youngest player to be selected for England Schoolboys, playing against a Scotland team that included Alan Hansen who would go on to make a name for himself as a footballer. He became Shropshire Boys Champion at the age of 15 in

A view of the re-developed Hawkstone Hotel from the golf course.

1973 at Market Drayton, beating a small lad called Ian Woosnam into second place. Ian Woosnam's club was near Oswestry and the two of them would meet up and play at Hawkstone and Oswestry alternately, a good match for each other and they became lifelong friends.

In 1973 Sandy Lyle ventured out to join the big boys and at the age of 15 just missed by two strokes from qualifying for the British Open at Troon where he watched and was inspired by Peter Thomson and Jack Nicklaus.

But the following year he became the youngest to ever qualify for the British Open at Royal Lytham and had the courage to ask the legendary Gary Player to play with him in the practices before the tournament proper. He was 16 and was about to leave Wem Secondary School when the Headmaster sent him a good luck telegram, and the local newspaper the *Shropshire Star* ran a major feature on him.

In the Open he played well for two rounds and actually made the cut before having a bad round and slipping down the field. Afterwards Gary Player who was the winner was asked about Lyle's potential. He said, 'He has the character and the guts to become a champion.' How prophetic were those words.

Sandy Lyle left Wem Secondary School in 1974 and worked for his father as a trainee green keeper and dogsbody in preparation for his apprenticeship as golf professional. The winter was hard but there was always work to do and his father was close by, encouraging and coaching him.

The honours started to come his way. He won the English Boys Stroke-Play Championship and became the youngest ever winner of the Brabazon, English Amateur Stroke-Play Championship, beating a certain young Nick Faldo.

Hawkstone Golf Club was developing well and in 1975 a celebrity match was arranged to inaugurate the opening of Weston, a new 18-hole course. Young Sandy Lyle found himself partnering the great Billy Wright and together they beat Martin Poxon and Joe Mercer.

With some great excitement and even more trepidation Sandy Lyle was offered and accepted a golf scholarship at the University of Houston in January 1976. He was apprehensive, he was dyslexic and he was nervous at starting to learn in an entirely new environment. His fears were justified: the golf was terrible and the lessons even worse and within three weeks he was home, followed shortly afterwards by Nick Faldo who had also accepted the same offer.

After several more successes in the amateur ranks, Lyle turned professional in 1977, aged 19, after achieving his one remaining ambition to represent Great Britain in the Walker Cup against America at Long Island.

He won his ticket for the European Tour and with many tournaments in Scotland he took the decision that from now on as a professional he would play for and be recognised as Scottish. He was the last player allowed to change his nationality in this fashion.

He had a contract with Dunlop and the financial backing of the Hawkstone Board of Directors and was taken under the management wing of Derek Pillage. His first big event was the

Argentine Open where he finished a creditable 6th, then he came home to spend that Christmas at Hawkstone. The week after his 20th birthday celebrations at the house, he left for Africa where he won his first professional title, the Nigerian Open.

Lyle started to make a reputation for himself in his new career very quickly and in 1979 and again in 1980, he won the European Tour Order of Merit. It was around this time that his manager Derrick Pillage introduced him to a young attractive professional female golfer, Christine Trew, and very soon after their first meeting they became engaged. They married on 24 October 1981 with the reception at Hawkstone Park Hotel before setting off to Hawaii for their honeymoon. They had two children, Stuart in 1983 and James in 1986, but the marriage fell on difficult times. It is a lonely life for many a professional golfer, continuously on the road, being self-centred and focussing only on winning. Many a marriage has been compromised. Even though Christine tried travelling all over the world with him, it was a difficult time and sadly in 1987 they agreed to part.

It was during this unsettling marital period that Sandy Lyle enjoyed some of his greatest successes. He represented Scotland in the World Team tournament first of all in 1979, then in 1980 where he won the individual title and again in 1987.

Apart from winning a Major, the greatest achievement for any golfer is to represent Europe in the Ryder Cup and Lyle was first selected to play in 1979 in West Virginia and again in 1981 in England as well as in Florida in 1983 – sadly all losing teams. But then in 1985 he was a member of the European team who after many years finally won back the Ryder Cup at the Belfry. This success was repeated in 1987 when he was a member of the European team that successfully defended the Cup on American soil in Ohio.

During this time he became the first Briton to win the British Open in sixteen years when he won at Royal St George's in 1985.

But 1987 was to bring him great success, not only in his professional life but also in his personal life. His upset at the break-up of his marriage was eased when he struck up a relationship with Jolande, a Dutch masseuse on the European Tour. During the Spanish Open their romance blossomed. Professionally meanwhile, he took part in a unique event when at Wentworth he lost in the final of the 1987 World Matchplay Championship to his fellow Salopian and long-time friend Ian Woosnam, a repeat of their meeting in 1973 at Market Drayton for the Shropshire Boys title, but with a reversal of the result. The year culminated in Sandy Lyle accompanied by his parents attending Buckingham Palace to receive the MBE and weeks later he was invited to lunch with her Majesty.

Arguably however his greatest professional achievement was still to come when in 1988 he won one of the greatest tournaments in the world and in so doing became the first Briton to win the event. He won the US Masters at Augusta and was awarded the much-coveted green jacket and as a result would automatically be accepted as a competitor at the annual tournament for life. He was regarded as the best player in the world and was proud to be part of the much-heralded 'Big 5' of European golf: all giants of their time, they were Lyle, Nick Faldo, Severiano Ballesteros, Bernhard Langer and fellow Salopian, Ian Woosnam.

On 20 October 1989, he married Jolande and after a honeymoon in Gibraltar they moved to a country house at Dolphinton on the Scottish Borders. Daughter Lonneke was born in April 1993 and son Quintin in 1995, which appeared to give the Lyles everything that they could wish for but, in 1996, Sandy lost both his parents within six months of each other. It was a grievous loss as Sandy and his parents had always been very close.

In the 1990s, mysteriously his form as one of the great golfers of his day deserted him and, when he won the Italian Open in 1992 it was the last tournament win of his career to date.

It is one of the great mysteries of golf why Sandy Lyle's form deserted him so permanently. All golfers go through bad phases but his has lasted years.

He now lives in semi-retirement on a remote 700-acre estate at Balquhidder in Scotland, which probably revives his happy memories of Hawkstone: he shoots, rides and fishes. But at the age of 50, Lyle still yearns for further success on the golf course and has joined the Seniors Professional Golf Tour, teaming up once again with old friends, including Ian Woosnam.

Sandy Lyle's ambition is to be the Captain of the European Ryder Cup team in the future.

Scotland in particular has produced several world-class golfers and although Sandy Lyle was inducted into the Scottish Sports Hall of Fame in 2004, there is no escaping the fact that he is a Shropshire lad and has spent more than half of his life in the county. Perhaps it is time for a Shropshire Hall of Fame!

Signed portrait of Sandy Lyle that hangs in the Hawkstone Hotel golf clubhouse, depicting Lyle's 1985 triumph in the British Open Champtonship.

140

Ian Woosnam 1958-

Shropshire-born Woosnam became the next Salopian to be classed as the world's best golfer during his playing career. A lifetime of travelling around the world, houses in Jersey and Barbados, a private plane and immortality in the history of world golf seemed a far cry from his upbringing on a small struggling dairy farm in Oswestry.

He was expected to play his part to support the family. His day would start with milking at 5am, moving and stacking bales of hay, driving tractors, mucking out and harvesting. There was always something to do and most days started very early and finished at around 10.30pm. Ian recalled, 'It was a tough life on the farm but it was also a lot of fun.' He once bemoaned the fact that today's children, with all their high-tech gadgets, seldom take to the outdoors as he did in his time: 'We used to go looking for bird's nests, fishing, swimming in the river, all that sort of thing.'

Although he was only small, he was a tough kid and enjoyed boxing and often when the family would go on holiday at Butlin's, when he was around seven years old, he would take on bigger kids and win holidays as a prize. The farm life toughened and strength-ened him. It was also around this time that he found that he had an aptitude for sport. He was a good soccer player and he started to play golf at seven years of age.

His local club, Llanymynech in Powys, is right on the Shropshire border and uniquely has fifteen of its holes in Wales with the other three in Shropshire! To reach the club is an achieve-ment in itself, coming out of the village and climbing the hill before taking a turn towards the club and ascending up the narrowest lanes I have ever encountered, very steep and very narrow, barely a car width. However on reaching the top and turning into the modest clubhouse grounds, the views are absolutely stunning and one can see the attraction immediately.

Llanymynech Golf Club where Woosnam began his golfing career. The course is unique in that 15 holes are in Wales and three are in Shropshire.

By the age of 14, Ian Woosnam was a county standard footballer and golfer and one weekend he was selected for Shropshire at both sports and had to make a choice. He later admitted, 'In my head I wanted to be a millionaire and I wanted to win major championships. So I chose golf.'

When I visited the club I was pleased to meet a young employee, Stewie, who knew the Woosnam family very well and who told me that when Ian was a young lad he used to practice golf by hitting the golf ball out of the ruts of ploughed fields and that it was this form of practise that eventually was to lead to him being regarded as one of golf's best ever iron players.

Just down the road at Hawkstone was another schoolboy golf prodigy Sandy Lyle and the two of them would meet up and play against one another, inspiring each other with a rivalry and a friendship that would last a lifetime.

He had some success as an amateur and he met Lyle when they were both 15 in 1973 at Market Drayton for the Shropshire Boys

Championship, but lost the title to his friend. Fourteen years later they would contest the final of the 1987 World Matchplay Championship at Wentworth but this time Woosnam would triumph.

When Woosnam was contemplating joining the ranks of the professional golfers, his many friends and colleagues advised him against it. Nevertheless, he turned professional in 1978 and for a while toured the European events in a battered rusty old mini-van with a couple of pals, existing on beans and whatever they could scavenge: the van was their home, eating, sleeping, wooing the girls. One of those friends, D.J. Russell, eventually went into business in later life with Woosnam, designing golf courses. In those early days, life was tough, with little success: one year the total prize money was £284!

It has been calculated that in those first five years of travelling the circuit, he earned only £6,000 – but his faith was unshakeable and in 1982 he won his first professional title, the Swiss Open, and was on his way to fame and riches.

By 1987 he was in the big league and that season he became the first European to win a million dollars by winning eight tournaments and won the World Matchplay Championship. His successes continued the following year when he won the British PGA Championship and in 1989 he was the individual winner in the World Cup team tournament. By 1991 he was ranked officially the number one player in the world and topped it off by winning the ultimate title, the US Masters at Augusta, and like Lyle before him was awarded the coveted green jacket entitling him to compete in the Augusta Masters for the rest of his life.

His winning streak continued in a whole variety of competitions, European tournaments and internationals. Despite being born in Shropshire, he represented Wales in the World Cup, the birthplace of his parents. Ian regards himself, and always has, as a Welshman.

Woosnam was a phenomenon because, in a sport in which height can be so vital in perfecting a powerful drive, he was only

5ft 4in tall! Despite what many experts regarded as a handicap, Woosnam was renowned as a long driver and the secret it was said lay in the smoothness of his swing. The great Ballesteros called his swing the 'sweetest in Europe' and his Shropshire friend Sandy Lyle perhaps more colourfully described his secret thus: 'Woosie combined Popeye's power with Fred Astaire's poise.'

He also had the distinction of being in the great European Ryder Cup Team that stopped the American domination of the event, being selected for the bi-annual contest from 1983 to 1995, an astonishing record of consistency in which the Europeans lost only one of the matches.

Similarly to Sandy Lyle, he had a loss of form in the 1990s and his last win of any significance was the Volvo PGA in 1997 but briefly in 2001 he had a mini-renaissance. At Wentworth he won the Cisco World Matchplay tournament and at the age of 43, established a record of winning this prestigious event in three decades: 1987, 1990 and 2001.

In the British Open at Lytham in the same year he hit the headlines but for all the wrong reasons. Going into the third round he was heading the leader board and seemed to have regained much of his old flair when it was discovered that he had too many clubs in his bag and he was penalised two strokes. The error, down to his caddie, cost him the Open that he had long cherished winning and he finished a highly creditable but frustrated third.

In 2002, he was appointed vice captain of the Ryder Cup squad that once again beat America and in 2006 received the ultimate accolade of being a most popular winning captain of the European Ryder Cup Team and in 2007 he was awarded the O.B.E for his services to British golf.

At the age of 50 in 2008 he became eligible to play in the Senior's Golf Tour, once again renewing his old rivalry with long-time friend Sandy Lyle, and not only did he win in Poland, his first win for 11 years, but he finished the season as No 1 in the Seniors ranks.

The little lad who dreamt of becoming a millionaire became a little man, but also a giant in his profession, respected by all who know him.

Richie Woodhall 1968-

Boxer Richie Woodhall is unquestionably a Salopian because from the age of two he was brought up in the county he is proud to call home and he is renowned in his community for the time that he devotes to local charities.

In 1971, his family moved to the corporation housing development at Warrens Way, Woodside, Telford and Ritchie remembers happy days playing in the streets. He recalls a happy childhood with plenty of friends enjoying football, cricket and in his particular case, going to the boxing gym from the age of six.

He was educated firstly at the William Reynolds Infants and Junior School, and then the Abraham Darby School, but he was always pleased to get home and enjoy outside activities with all his pals. Those friends have stayed with him from those very early days, even to the extent that more than twenty of them followed him to Washington for his first, but unsuccessful, shot at a world title against the American boxer Keith Holmes.

Richie Woodhall has said on more than one occasion how grateful he is for the experience that being brought up in Shropshire's Woodside area gave him and it is true to say that his sense of community was engendered by the example of his father who devoted much of his time to teaching the young lads in the neighbourhood. His father believed that boxing taught young people control, discipline and respect and he influenced many a local youngster away from trouble and crime to follow a path of decency. Richie Woodhall today uses his fame in a similar way to his father, in his own community efforts.

As Ritchie entered his teens he became a useful boxer but he took the next step up in class when he represented Great Britain at the 1988 Seoul Olympics and brought back an Olympic bronze medal. He was now seen as a prospective professional champion and duly in 1990, after winning the Commonwealth Games gold medal in Auckland, New Zealand, he joined the ranks of the paid fighters.

From 1992 until 1995 he was the undefeated Commonwealth Middleweight champion and from 1995 until late 1996 he was the undefeated European champion. Eventually on an unforgettable night for the 4,000 or so supporters packed into the Telford Ice Rink stadium in 1998, he became the WBC World Super-Middleweight champion by defeating Sugar Boy Malinga.

Shortly afterwards he had a dispute with his manager Frank Warren and was inactive in the ring for more than eight months and when the time came for him to defend his title in 1999, he lost it to Marcus Beyer, a man he was expected to have beaten. In 2001 he fought for the WBO Super-Middleweight against good friend and boxing legend Joe Calzaghe and lost again and sadly his career as a top class fighter was over.

Richie Woodhall, unlike some boxers, has managed to adjust to life outside the fighting ring. He is married to wife Jayne and they have three children but Richie admits he doesn't want the boys to follow him into boxing, as he couldn't bear to see them hurt! That coming from a fighting man but spoken like a loving father.

The family live near Ironbridge on a self-build development with the same feeling of community spirit that he grew up to appreciate. Nearby is his Ironbridge Gorge Power Station boxing gym and he has recently featured in the establishment of a boxing gym for youngsters in Aston, Birmingham. He also assisted the local council with the regeneration of his old housing estate at Woodside, determined to put back into the sport some of the positive experiences that brought him so much respect and affection. He

146

is articulate, passionate and modest, all qualities that have assisted him in becoming a respected boxing commentator with the BBC today, as well as his recent appointment to the Olympic Boxing Training squad for 2012.

In a recent interview he revealed that his feet were very firmly fixed to the ground when he confessed that his career success was very much down to his upbringing on the council estate at Woodside and irrespective of some of the more glamorous aspects to his fame and celebrity, he said that he likes nothing more than settling down in a local pub in Telford, chatting to some of the older folks about the old days in Madeley or Dawley. He is still today a professional boxing trainer but is also a well-rounded, much-respected figure: a former world champion and a very worthy Salopian.

Chapter Six

MURDER MOST FOUL

Since the dawn of civilisation, murder has been the ultimate crime: man's evil solution to the frustrations created by greed, fear, jealousy or passion. Despite greater education, despite all the deterrents and punishments, the act of murder will regrettably dog mankind until the end of time.

Murder can never be condoned but on occasions can be understood, where reason has been overtaken by the basic instincts of fear, revenge or an attempt to protect vulnerable loved ones. However, there are instances where murder is so brutal, so heinous, so sadistic, so horrific and pre-meditated, it defies all understanding.

Shropshire, like every other county in Great Britain, has had its share of brutal murders, many of which have made headline news.

The last man hanged in Shrewsbury

A young butcher's assistant has the dubious distinction of being the last man to be hanged for murder in Shrewsbury. Until the very last minute there was hope of a reprieve, but it was not forthcoming and at the age of 21 George Riley from Copthorne became the last man to be hanged in Shrewsbury. Much of the evidence against him was circumstantial and his alleged signed confession, which he later denied, was held to be what damned him.

The events unfolded on a Friday night in October 1960 when George came home from work and dutifully handed over to his mother his contribution to the household bills out of his weekly wage.

That night he went out on the town with a friend and consumed a fair amount of drink before moving on to a dance at Harlescott where Riley got involved in several minor fights in what was proving to be a lively night out. However, there were two off-duty policeman at the dance who later opined that Riley was not drunk.

His friend drove Riley home at about 1.30am and Riley claimed that he could not get into the house as he had not taken a key with him and settled down for the night on a settee in the garage. He would later claim that he woke up, saw the dining room light on in the house and was let in by his brother Terry, went to bed and fell asleep. In the morning it was observed that his trousers were marked green in places from grass stains and his shoes were muddy.

The morning erupted into chaos when screams pierced the air and police were seen rushing into a house across the street, belonging to a widow Mrs Smith, who was known to Riley. Mrs Smith's sister had telephoned her and, when unable to get a reply, had called round in person, but was unable to gain access and called the police for assistance. A sergeant noticed that a pane of glass in the french windows had been broken and was able to get at the latch and lift it to enable entry. When Mrs Smith's sister entered the house and went into her sister's bedroom, her screams reverberated around the small street. Mrs Smith's battered, semi-naked body was lying on the floor in a pool of blood with her face and head savagely beaten and with a number of her teeth missing; she had been subjected to a brutal assault.

Riley was questioned and later at his trial his defence successfully argued that his first statement was inadmissible as he had not been advised of his rights and that in any case he had not signed the statement. However, he did write out a second statement with altered facts but still to all intents and purposes an admission of guilt, allegedly saying, 'I am signing my death warrant, aren't I?'

He said that he had entered her house in a drunken state seeking money, which he knew from previous visits that she sometimes kept around the house. When she saw him she sat up in bed and in her panic grasped him. He admitted he hit her hard in the face and continued punching, causing her great damage, mainly because of a large ring on one of his fingers. He claimed that he had no other motive other than money, but no money had been taken and tragically the widow had only three shillings and seven and a half pence in her purse; a pittance.

Riley said that he had panicked and ran across the fields before returning home, hence the muddy shoes and grass-stained trousers. Experts suggest that today it would be difficult to convict him, despite the circumstantial evidence, because he later suggested that the confession had been prompted by the police and it was certainly said to have been well-written. In addition, there was no money taken, no finger-print evidence and no motive. However, the circumstantial evidence, together with Riley's comments, indicated that the police had no need to look further for a killer.

The Black Panther

The whole of Great Britain was shocked by a callous and brutal murder in 1975, perpetrated by a small-time crook who had evolved into a dangerous full-blown criminal. It involved a 17-year-old girl from the village of Highley, Shropshire.

Donald Nappey was born in 1936 and after an uneventful early life spent as a handyman and self employed builder working in the Yorkshire area, he turned to burglary. Then for almost 15 years he got away with a whole series of robberies specialising in post office hold-ups. He began to believe that he was invincible, planning his operations with military precision and proving to be ruthless whenever confronted or thwarted.

By the time he reached Kidsgrove, Staffordshire, where he would commit the vilest of his crimes, he had shot and killed three sub-postmasters in Harrogate, Accrington and Langley. He believed that the planning and geographical spread of his targets would make it difficult for him to be traced and for a time he was correct. He was now acquiring a degree of arrogance and changed his name from Nappey to Neilson. He was also nicknamed 'The Black Panther' by the media because of the dark-coloured balaclava he wore during his robberies.

On a visit to Kidsgrove he was attracted by the potential of the Bath Pool valley area that had once been the hub of the local mining industry and was riddled with drainage shafts linked to old workings and was not overlooked by residents. It was now a more tranquil landscaped facility and he noticed that there was easy access and exit routes close to the network of old mine shafts. It would be ideal for the purpose he had in mind.

January 1975, a 17-year-old girl was spending some time during her Christmas break from Wulfrun College, Wolverhampton, at her family home in Highley, Shropshire. Lesley Whittle's father had died

151

in 1970, leaving her £82, 000 he had accrued from a very successful Shropshire/Worcestershire coach business. It was hoped that Lesley and her brother Ronald would one day inherit the business.

Neilson knew about the wealth of the family and regarded her as a potential source of income. On the night of 14 January he drove to Highley, crept into the sleeping girl's bedroom and kidnapped her. After driving to the Bath Pool site, he forced her to descend a drainage shaft he had previously identified, into the pitch-black darkness. He placed a wire around her neck, tied her hands and left the terrified girl with a sleeping bag and some food, to dwell on her fate.

Next morning her poor mother went upstairs when Lesley had not appeared for breakfast, found her daughter's bed empty and spotted three Dymotape-label messages in the sitting room, one saying, 'If police or tricks, death.' There was also a demand for £50,000, together with instructions as to where and how the ransom was to be delivered.

That same night there was an incident which would later prove absolutely crucial to finding Leslie – and if it had been appreciated and pursued at the time, there might have been a happier outcome. Neilson had stolen a Green Morris 1300 and whilst finalising details of the kidnap plot, he shot a security guard at the Dudley Freight-liner Depot carpark who had come to investigate. He abandoned the car, but it was only investigated some seven weeks later. In it was found a tape-recorded message from Lesley Whittle giving detailed instructions for the delivery of the cash.

Despite Neilson's instructions, the family decided to confide in the police and on 16 January, with the knowledge of the police, Lesley's brother Ronald set out to follow the trail.

Ronald left Bridgnorth police station heading for Kidsgrove, an area unfamiliar to him and as a result the journey took longer than expected. Despite his detailed planning, Nielson had been too clever. One set of instructions were hidden in a telephone box and after finding this and heading for Bath Pool, Ronald missed the next instruction left beside a flashing torch. By now he was later than the instructions demanded so he decided to abort the mission and continued driving past Bath Pool. Ironically, he was very close to where his sister Lesley was hidden.

All contacts between the Whittles and Neilson were severed and for some weeks the mystery of the fate of the young girl perplexed police and the public. However, local people at Bath Pool discovered a torch, strips of Dymo-tape, one of which was attached to a tree bearing the message: 'Drop suitcase in Hole'. The Green Morris was finally investigated and all clues pointed to Bath Pool.

On 6 March, eight weeks since Lesley had been kidnapped, a full-scale search of the area was organised and eventually the disused mineshaft was discovered. Hanging from a ledge with a steel wire around her throat was the lifeless body of the young 17-year-old. It was a truly shocking end to a callous kidnapping. It was unclear from the evidence whether Neilson had deliberately hanged the young girl or whether she had slipped from the ledge. However, what was clear was that Neilson could not have afforded to let her go once his plans had gone awry.

The national newspapers broke the news to a horrified public and in the belief that the murderer might have been a local man with knowledge of the mining area, a massive interview process was launched involving 3,000 men from the Kidsgrove area.

Months went by without any significant developments and it was Neilson himself who brought life back into the investigation.

Once a crook, always a crook.

In December 1975 he reverted once again to armed robbery. Whilst researching a potential robbery site in Mansfield, he attracted the attention of police officers who started to question him. A struggle ensued in which Neilson pulled his gun and attempted to shoot the officers before they overpowered him.

While in custody, Neilson refused to answer questions, but

when the police searched his home in Leeds they found damning evidence: firearms, a blue balaclava helmet that was later confirmed by forensic scientists to have been the one sprayed with ammonia during one of his robberies and a Dymo-tape labeller that matched the labels found at Bath Pool.

The evidence was compelling and Neilson, the self-styled Black Panther, the callous murderer of a defenceless schoolgirl and the killer of three sub-postmasters, was found guilty on 14 June 1976 and received life sentences for each of the murders as well as for abduction and armed robbery. He was incarcerated in a high-security prison where he still languishes today.

The murder devastated the Whittle family who were well known in the Shropshire area and horrified local people who found it difficult to come to terms with such callous, pre-meditated cruelty on their door-step.

British Secret Service agents murder Shropshire woman?

On 24 March 1984, West Mercian police finally found the body of Hilda Murrell, a well-known Shropshire woman, who had been missing for several days. The body, with four stab wounds, had been dumped by a tree in a lane next to a Shrewsbury farmer's land. The cause of death was the wounds and hypothermia.

There followed a chain of events more akin to an Agatha Christie mystery, and twenty years after her murder, the crime remained unsolved until 2005.

Hilda Murrell was born in Shrewsbury in 1906 and, after an education at Cambridge, she chose to join the very successful family business of nurserymen, florists and seedsmen which had been founded in 1837. She quickly proved to be an asset and in 1937 became the Business & Horticultural Director of Edwin Murrell Ltd. After the war, in which she became much respected for her charitable work, the business went from strength to strength and she became internationally known as an expert on roses and their propagation. Her firm competed in all the major flower shows, Chelsea, Southport and of course Shrewsbury, and supplied roses to the Queen Mother and the Churchill family.

She was particularly interested in the environment and was a great enthusiast of the Shropshire countryside and its wildlife, fiercely protecting and promoting its conservation. She was a founder member of the National Soil Association, championing organic horticulture. Murrell was also an expert botanist and something of an artist which she demonstrated when her edited *Nature Diaries 1961-83* were published to great acclaim.

In 1970 she decided to retire and sold the family business to a gentleman who would go on to make a name for himself in the same genre, Percy Thrower.

Now with more time to devote to her multifarious interests, Hilda became increasingly passionate about conserving Shropshire's heritage, particularly its medieval architecture. She was also vociferously opposed to nuclear energy. After the almost-disastrous accident at the American nuclear plant at Three Mile Island in 1979, she wrote a critical article 'What Price Nuclear Power?' and later another article highly critical of the 1982 Government White Paper on 'Radioactive Waste Management'.

She was an active anti-nuclear campaigner, a supporter of the Greenham Common women's resistance to American Cruise missiles and was highly critical of Prime Minister Thatcher's friendship with America in return for its nuclear protection. She was vehemently opposed to the proposed nuclear plant at Sizewell in Suffolk, based on the same design as that which failed at Three Mile Island. All in all, she was an acknowledged thorn in the side of the Establishment and her views were widely-known and would play a part in attempting to solve the mystery of her murder.

Following her murder, the case became more convoluted. Hilda Murrell's nephew Commander Robert Green was an intelligence officer working in London during the Falklands War and answerable to Admiral Sir John Fieldhouse, Commander-in-Chief Fleet. Commander Green was suspected of leaking confidential information to Labour politician Thomas 'Tam' Dalyell on the sinking of the *General Belgrano*, the Argentine cruiser, by the British nuclear submarine *HMS Conqueror*. The sinking of the ship was a political hot potato, with allegations of a cover-up and 'edited' official reports.

However, in December 1984, Dalyell told the House of Commons that, although his information had not come from Commander Green, he alleged that Green had sent the order to sink the *Belgrano*. He was wrong on two counts: intelligence officers have no jurisdiction in ordering attacks and Commander Green wasn't even on duty that night.

Tam Dalyell then launched a bombshell. He alleged that British Secret Service intelligence officers had been sent to Hilda Murrell's house to search for any incriminating papers that Commander Green might have given to his aunt for concealment about the sinking of the General Belgrano. He went on to imply that whilst they were searching her property, she had probably disturbed them.

Another line of enquiry opened up when allegations emerged that anti-nuclear activists, particularly those objecting to the Sizewell project, were being investigated by the Secret Service. Dirty deeds were suspected when Don Arnott, a respected British radio-chemist who had suggested that he knew what had caused the meltdown on Three Mile Island, suddenly dropped out of the Sizewell campaign after suffering a mysterious heart attack! Just six weeks before her death, Hilda had had a meeting with him.

Motives for Hilda Murrell's murder abounded, including the highly controversial allegations that she was silenced by British Secret Service or murdered by agents seeking to demotivate the anti-nuclear lobby. Over the ensuing years, speculation continued in a series of books, plays, television documentaries, magazine and newspaper articles but the mystery remained unsolved until 2005.

Advances in the science of forensics, especially diagnostic techniques on DNA, had resulted in the solving of a number of long-term crimes. Old cases were re-opened and re-examined in the light of the new techniques.

Around 2003 interest in the Hilda Murrell case was revised as the police had one piece of evidence still in their possession, an underskirt of the victim's with semen stains on it. Applying the new forensic techniques, the police then reviewed more than 3,000 statements recorded in their earlier investigations.

The new evidence led to the arrest of 35-year-old labourer Andrew George at his home in Harlescott, Shrewsbury. At the time of the murder, he was a 16-year-old living in a children's home with his brother.

At the trial the court heard that he had broken into Murrell's house looking for money, tied her to the banisters, sexually assaulted her and then stabbed her three times. He then dragged her into her own car and drove for 6 miles before stabbing her again and dumping her body in the woods. George blamed the murder on his brother but there was no evidence for this and he was found guilty of murder and jailed in 2005 for life.

After more than 20 years of claim and counter-claim, of conspiracy theories of Secret Service involvement and nefarious inferences from political bodies, the crime turned out to be, simply, an opportunist burglary, shocking in so much as it involved a 16-year-old torturing, sexually assaulting and murdering a highly respected 78-year-old woman.

Murder at Heath House

An unsolved murder that occurred in the sleepy village of Hopton Heath, south Shropshire, in 1987, would have thwarted any editor or film producer seeking a plausible plot. The crime had all the intrigue, the exotic characters and the twisted chain of events of the most implausible detective thriller. A country mansion, a young wife, a seedy, faded European aristocrat, a haughty Baroness, a link to King Arthur, missing gold bars, the fraud of a titled Lady, a body found in a pool of blood, killed from behind by a long narrow object (poker or candlestick?) and a chief suspect who treats the police with contempt and who is found not guilty: couldn't possibly happen? Well, it happened in Shropshire.

Susan Wilberforce, a distant relative of William Wilberforce, renowned for his efforts to abolish slavery, met and married architect Simon Dale in London in 1957.

She was fifteen years younger than the 38-year-old Dale and from a wealthy, more aristocratic background: finishing school in Paris, large country houses, her father a Lieutenant Colonel killed in the Second World War, a non-maternal mother and a closer relationship with her auntie Lady Illingworth. Her upbringing created in her a degree of reticence, bordering on aloofness. Dale was middle class and not only brought Susan a degree of stability but she, he thought, would open her world to him and assist him in obtaining clients in his business of restoring old country houses.

In 1959 the couple bought, with Susan's money, a run-down, isolated and vast country home, Heath House, at Hopton Heath near Ludlow. In a beautiful but remote part of the countryside, it required considerable renovation to make it more hospitable.

For more than ten years they were almost reclusive in their country retreat. Neighbours were few and far between and anyway they didn't mix with neighbours. For a time they seemed content to bring up their five children.

However, by the end of the 1960s the marriage was collapsing. Business was very poor, Dale's eyesight was failing and according to Susan there were many arguments, often violent. They lived apart within the large house and for most of the time their children were away at schools; it was a miserable existence. Eventually they divorced in 1972 and Heath House was put on the market with an agreement to divide the profit equally.

Probably because of its remoteness, Heath House attracted no purchasers and for fifteen years Simon and Susan lived hand-to-mouth. Susan moved to a smaller house in Docklow, near Leominster, taking the younger children with her but they also remained in contact with their father.

Life for Simon was miserable in the extreme, alone in the large house that had once rung with the sound of children and laughter; it was now a dank, soulless tomb. Children's toys remained scattered around, there were dozens of chilly unoccupied rooms: it was a home with the heart ripped out of it. He lived in the kitchen and slept in a four-poster bed but, despite his circumstances, he was loath to leave.

He believed that the house was a site of historic interest and at one time he claimed that he had found the foundations of Camelot and told the newspapers that he was writing books on the subject and wanted it preserved, with himself as curator. Susan was of course desperate for the proceeds from any sale and he was showing little interest in selling. The few neighbours that he had were supportive of him and although they regarded him as eccentric, they liked him and said that far from being violent, they found him to be a gentle man, if a little strange.

In the early 1980s another character emerges. The seedy European aristocrat Baron Michael Victor Jossif de Stempel reappeared in Susan's life. She had had an affair with him before

Heath House at Hopton Heath, the scene of Dale's murder in 1987.

marrying Simon. He was rakish, arrogant and had at one time in their affair had asked her to marry him, but she had refused and it was while he was away in South America that she met and fell in love with Simon Dale; a far different partner.

Susan and the Baron now resumed their affair. Meanwhile Susan's wealthy aunt, Lady Illingworth, who lived in a mansion suite and suffered with senile dementia, came into the plot. Susan's daughter Sophia was living with Lady Illingworth whilst working as a secretary and in February 1984 she brought Lady Illingworth with her to Docklow for a holiday break.

It is not known when Lady Illingworth fell victim to her niece's scheming but Susan believed that her mother and Lady Illingworth had both favoured her brother John in their wills and that she stood to get very little.

Within days of her aunt's visit, Susan, supported and perhaps encouraged by Baron de Stempel, had accessed Lady Illingworth's bank accounts, obtained share certificates, set up a new will in which Susan was the main beneficiary. She obtained antiques, paintings and other valuables from her London apartment, storage and bank safe-keeping, and sold them all at auctions – netting around one million pounds.

However, it was also rumoured that Lady Illingworth had in her possession a number of gold bars, a story which was re-enforced when a removal man later told the police that he had seen the gold bars in the cellar of Lady Illingworth's previous house in Grosvenor Square.

The fraud was breathtakingly greedy and audacious and in just a few months they had Lady Illingworth consigned to a Hereford nursing home, claiming that she was too ill for them to cope with. They had bled her dry, spending her money on a car and a flat in Spain. In 1984, Susan and Michael married and she became Baroness de Stempel but within the year they had parted, leaving Susan heart-broken. The Baron had been unable to change his ways and had indulged in extra marital activities. In all, he would marry three times.

Lady Illingworth died in 1986. She had requested to be buried next to her husband at the Illingworth family tomb in Bradford but with no respect for her wishes, she was cremated and her relations were only notified after the event.

For a time Susan and Baron de Stempel must have thought that they had got away with the defrauding of Lady Illingworth or Aunt Puss as they called her.

Alone now with her children, Susan continued with her determination to have Heath House sold and she became a regular visitor there, spending time attempting to renovate and improve the look of the property and its grounds. She also removed furniture from time to time that she considered to be hers. On occasions Simon would object to her presence, complaining that he was being harassed. Harsh words would be exchanged.

The whole tragic and sorry story came to a climax when on 13 September 1987 Giselle Wall, a friend of Simon Dale, had to force open the door to his kitchen. The horrified woman found his body lying in a pool of blood. His skull had been battered with a heavy object and he was dead. There was food still cooking in the oven, giving the murder scene a disarming sense of normality.

When the police visited Docklow to break the shocking news of Simon's murder to the family, they were astonished at the total indifference of his former wife and children.

Police continued with their enquiries but Susan was almost contemptuous of them and she bragged to Baron de Stempel in a letter how she had lectured these 'little men' on her nobility. During their enquiries the police uncovered the fraud perpetrated on Lady Illingworth. Susan and two of her children, Marcus and Sophia, were immediately charged with the murder of Simon Dale. However within days the murder charge against Sophia and Marcus had been dropped although they were still charged with assisting their mother with the fraud.

When the murder trial opened at Worcester, the prosecution had both motive and opportunity, but there was very little hard evidence to pin the murder on Baroness de Stempel. A crowbar was found at the cottage which had been used by Susan, Marcus and Sophia when visiting Heath House, but it had been cleaned and contained no implicating stains.

Throughout her two days in the witness box, Susan, Baroness de Stempel was imperious, dismissing with graceful arrogance any suggestion that she murdered her husband. She would not be intimidated by the QC and frequently berated him, dismissing one of his assertions with 'Bollocks, Mr Palmer'. Calm and collected, she had an answer for everything and skilfully deflected difficult questions or was disarmingly honest with others. She won the jury over and was found not guilty.

She did, however, plead guilty to defrauding Lady Illingworth and received a seven year sentence for that. Marcus and Sophia claimed that they had been unwitting tools but still received

18 months and 30 months respectively and Baron de Stempel, despite his protestations that he was just helping when in fact his knowledge was vital in forging and setting up banking details and wills, received a four year sentence.

Typically Baron de Stempel dismissed the verdict thus: 'It was about what I would have expected from a working-class jury.'

The mystery of the missing gold bars remained and there was a suggestion that they had been moved from the cellar at some time and lodged in the vaults of the Natwest Bank. Further research revealed the intriguing note on the bank's inventory 'Boxes, very heavy'.

During their prison sentences, all four of the guilty parties received letters from solicitors dealing on behalf of Lady Illingworth's estate demanding the return of: '30 gold bars, each 18 inches long, with a total vale of £12 million pounds'. From where did they receive such detailed information? There was, however, no evidence of sudden wealth from Susan or her family and the police treated the matter lightly although they did organise a search of Heath House and dug up parts of the grounds in their futile efforts. No trace of the gold has ever been found.

Author Terry Kirby, who wrote a fascinating book on the case, *Trials of the Baroness*, got to know the family quite well in carrying out his research. He confirms that the Baroness was adamant that she did not murder her husband and he believes that, on coming out of prison, she was genuinely penniless.

She lived for a time in Wales and London and renewed her relationship with Baron Michael de Stempel although he lived most of the time with his second wife in London. During his research, Terry was shown around Heath House by Marcus who is now married and lives in Scotland; his sister Sophia is a secretary in London.

The murder remains unsolved to this day although conjecture continues. Was a hit-man used? Was it a murder by a robber seeking antiques in an old mansion? Did someone come seeking the gold ingots?

The police have never sought to re-open the case and it may never be solved.

Heath House was eventually sold in 1993 and the proceeds used to pay off Baroness de Stempel's considerable debts.

Behind Closed Doors

In August 2008 the nation was shocked by the terrible tragedy that unfolded in the small north Shropshire village of Maesbrook. To all intents and purposes, the Foster family, father Christopher 50, mother Jill 49 and 15-year-old daughter Kirstie, had the perfect lifestyle. Their five bed-roomed 16th century home, Osbaston House, worth more than a million pounds, was set in 15 acres with its own stables, horses, dogs and a fleet of luxury cars, all trappings of the wealthy businessman Foster purported to be.

His pipe insulation business, Ulva Ltd, had been the basis of his fortune, providing the lavish lifestyle envied by many. However as the saying goes, 'no one knows what goes on behind closed doors'.

Foster's business was in trouble and by 2007 it was forced into administration. He was determined to maintain outward appearances although inwardly he was suffering considerably. He was about to go into liquidation, become bankrupt, owing millions. His animals, cars and house were on the brink of being repossessed.

He kept this information from his family although it is alleged that he had confided in his doctor that he was on the brink of suicide and, despite owning a firearms licence, nothing was done to remove it. He told a friend that he would kill himself rather than let the bailiffs in and told another that he could not bear the thought of his family learning of his problems and then having to surrender such a privileged lifestyle. Only the previous week his daughter Kirstie, a keen horse rider, had gained first place at the

Berriew Show. Clearly even this modicum of success put greater pressure on her father, emphasising that their comfortable lifestyle would very soon be changed forever. Christopher Foster, the failed business-man, was in torment.

For friends, family and neighbours there was little indication of the horror about to come as the family attended a neighbour's barbecue on the night of 25 August, 2008. The Fosters seemed fine, laughing and relaxing with their friends, but as they drove the short distance back to their own luxurious house, Foster knew that his creditors were closing in and he had made his mind up to end it all that night. CCTV footage showed the family arriving back at the house with young Kirstie rushing to check on her horses and being greeted by her excited dogs.

The atmosphere must have changed later that night because daughter Kirstie exchanged a series of texts with a friend as she sat up in bed, aimless teenage girl chat but at one point she confided that she was 'scared'. Her father had cut off her internet connection, presumably as a prequel to the activation of his awful scheme.

Sometime after 12.14am when Kirstie finished communicating with her friend, Christopher Foster crept into his daughter's room and shot her in the back of the head as she slept. Around the same time he went into his own bedroom and shot his sleeping wife in similar circumstances.

CCTV footage shows him after the killings, moving around the grounds of the estate, shooting the family's three horses and four dogs. His actions were all quite deliberate, such as when he moved a horse box to the main gates then shot out the tyres, making it very difficult for emergency services to gain access to the property. He then sprinkled kerosene around the house before starting four fires, two inside the house and two outside. After they were well ablaze, he calmly walked back into the burning house and lay down beside his wife, hoping to suffocate in the fumes and smoke.

By the time the Fire Brigade arrived the property was an

inferno and beyond saving. At first the services believed that they were dealing with a very severe house fire until the evidence slowly emerged that murder might have been involved. Two charred bodies were found, identified a couple of days later as belonging to Christopher and Jill but there was still no sign of Kirstie, giving rise to the theory that the Fosters may have been murdered and their daughter kidnapped. However. after six days of sifting through the rubble and smouldering remains, the remnants of what turned out to be a human body were eventually identified as that of young Kirstie.

When police were later able to consult the CCTV footage and talk to Christopher Foster's distraught mother, the horrific explanation for the terrible nights activities became clear.

Foster's disturbed state of mind had resulted in this terrible action of murdering a loving, supportive wife and a talented, attractive young daughter with everything to live for, indicating that he had been driven, however temporarily, insane with stress, shame and fear. Despite being a close loving family, he could not bear to live with the notion that he had let his family down. However, his estranged brother Andrew, who was now put in charge of the family's estate, had not spoken to Christopher for many years and believed that he was a dominant man who had to be in control and that the final act of destruction was a reflection of his true character.

Jill's family were devastated and understandably had little respect for Christopher Foster, branding his actions unforgivable. They insisted that he should not be buried with the wife and daughter he had just killed.

The coroner later declared a verdict of unlawful killing of Mrs Jill Foster and Kirstie by Christopher Foster who had afterwards committed suicide.

The Chip Shop Murders...
Two Men Battered

In October 2008 the West Midlands news carried a report of the murder of two men found dead in a flat above a fish and ship shop in the village of Shawbury. The murders had occurred in December 2007 above Mike's Fish Bar in a three-bed roomed flat occupied by illegal immigrants.

The owners of the flat were alerted to the situation following an 'excitable' phone call from another illegal immigrant, Sukhdev Singh, on 7 December, who had sought sanctuary in a Sikh temple.

When the police were called to the flat they found the bodies of 30-year-old Jaswant Singh Bajwa and 31-year-old Kulwant Singh Dodar. Jaswant worked in the chip shop but his friend Kulwant was just staying the night.

The post-mortem revealed that they had been battered to death with successive blows to the head from an object presumed to be a hammer. The struggle had ended on the stairs of the flat and both bodies were discovered lying at the bottom of the stairway.

On 11 December the police tracked Sukhdev down to the Sikh temple and although he claimed that he had merely discovered the dead bodies and had panicked and fled, the police arrested him.

Following further police investigations supported by forensic information, it was suggested to him that the murders had taken place in the flat and not on the stairs and it was he who had killed the two men and then dragged the bodies down the stairs to conceal his actions.

Sukhdev Singh confessed at Stafford Crown Court that he had murdered the two men before fleeing to the Sikh temple. No motive for the murders was ever proffered.

The Massage Parlour Murders

The inhabitants Frankwell, a suburb of Shrewsbury, had no idea of the struggle for life taking place in the local massage parlour that also acted as a brothel, one sunny July day in 2006.

Garry Harding, a 22-year-old from Welshpool, Powys had been a customer at the parlour, Rachel's Health Studio, and had used the additional facilities offered by the prostitutes in the past. However his visit on 1 July was not about sexual gratification but robbery. He believed that the women would make an easy target and he was desperate to try and somehow reduce his £16,000 gambling debts.

His crime was premeditated for he came to the parlour armed with a hammer and after discovering that the women were alone, he put his plan into action. The two women on duty that day were 55-year-old receptionist Annie Eels and 24-year-old prostitute Samantha Tapper. Little did they know that as they greeted him with a smile they would shortly be fighting, unsuccessfully, for their lives. Harding battered both women to death, leaving their brutalised bodies mangled on the parlour floor. At first there were few clues and the police had to track down, investigate and question regular customers of the brothel.

After a painstaking process in which eighteen officers were commended for their work in one of the biggest enquiries in the history of the West Mercian police, involving 300 officers, Garry Harding was identified as the major suspect. He continued, despite the evidence against him, to deny any involvement in the heinous crime but on the first day of his trial at Birmingham Crown Court in April 2007 he changed his plea to guilty.

It was a cold-blooded, merciless, premeditated killing of two defenceless women in a quiet part of Shrewsbury one sunny July day.

Chapter Seven

IT HAPPENED IN SHROPSHIRE... OR DID IT?

Ghosts, Paranormal Apparitions and Legends

For most people, ghosts do not exist except in the imagination of others. Those who are absolutely convinced that they have experienced something supernatural are invariably informed by others that the event is impossible and that the apparition is to do with some mechanism of the brain that we are yet to understand.

Some believers suggest that another dimension we have no knowledge of transports the images; while sceptics suggest that ghostly apparitions are down to an over-active imagination.

Whatever the truth, ghost hunting today is big business. There are various experts in the field, ranging from parapsychologists, paranormal investigators, mediums, séance conductors, ghost hunters and exorcists, some of whom now use the most advanced scientific equipment to validate their business. Through the use of ultra-modern technology they hope one day to make the breakthrough, perhaps to another world. Video cameras, backed up by the very latest still photography, electromagnetic field detectors tracing the movement of energy unseen by the human eye, ultraviolet light detectors and incredibly sensitive microphones make it extremely difficult to miss the movement of anything unless of course it is made from or comes from somewhere beyond our understanding.

Many of us I am sure have recounted ghost stories to each other in order to frighten or entertain, and films, books and stories of ghosts are forever popular.

I must declare my own position here as being a total sceptic.

Shropshire has the history, the geographical features and the wild characteristics which are sufficient to make it ideal ghost territory. It has over a thousand years of fighting, rebellion, torture, cruelty and unspeakable horrors foisted upon its population. Ancient burial grounds, dark and foreboding castles hinting at past terrors, fortified mansions, walled, medieval towns with sites of merciless public executions and a landscape fashioned over millennia and pitted with caverns, caves and old mine shafts lend credence to the belief in witches, demons and ghosts; restless from the horrors of the past.

For many centuries it was believed that at the Midwinter Solstice on Stiperstones Hill, the highest point in the county, evil spirits from all over the country came together on the hill. Close by Bishops Castle is the Lea Stone which, legend has it, was left by the Devil when he picked it out of his boot and threw it aside. Today, Bishops Castle has an active coven of white witches.

Over the centuries, mining activities for lead, iron ore, copper and coal has left behind many cavities, leaving the county riddled with caves and underground shafts.

When in 1070, Shropshire's Wild Edric made peace with William the Conqueror, many local people cursed him, believing that he had sold out to the devil. For centuries afterwards around the Stiperstones area, Wild Edric was said to appear from time to time as a huge hound with staring red eyes. He was also believed to have a ghostly secret army hidden away in the caves that only manifested itself in times of national emergency. At various times the ghostly army was claimed to have been seen, during the Napoleonic, Crimean, Boer and First World Wars.

Another legend linked to the Stiperstones is the Devil's Chair, a jagged rocky outcrop situated close to the top of the hill. On warm summer nights the smell of brimstone is to be sensed in the air indicating that Beelzebub is present and sitting on his throne, surveying the bleak landscape.

Local legends persist in the belief that if you spend a dark night sitting on the Devil's Chair you will be found the following morning either inspired or insane! Legend also has it that the Devil was filling in the valley at nearby Hell's Gutter with rocks and boulders when his apron strings snapped, causing him to drop the gathered rocks, leaving them where they still stand today.

However, another version of the story suggests that the Devil despised Shropshire and started accumulating the boulders in the hope that the county would eventually sink under the weight and disappear into the sea.

Wenlock Edge, particularly the area on the cliff between Presthope and Lutwyche Hall, is the haunt of the ghost of Old Ippikin. Ippikin was the leader of a gang of robbers who terrorised the area in the 13th century and who was distinguished by a long, protruding chin. Legend has it that anyone daring to stand on the cliff top and taunt Ippikin about his chin would be thrown from the cliff top. He accumulated a great deal of treasure from his robberies which he hid in a cave on Wenlock Edge.

One stormy night when he and his gang were sheltering in the cave, lightning dislodged a massive boulder that crashed down blocking the entrance and sealing Ippikin and his men inside. He is said to roam Wenlock Edge still, seeking victims to throw off the

171

cliff top. Ippikin's rock, the site where the cave was blocked, can be seen just above Upper Hill Farm.

There is a particularly appealing legend almost similar to a fairy tale concerning Stapeley Hill and a carving in the church at Middleton that refers to a time when the region was hit badly by drought. According to legend, as the people were close to starvation, a Fairy Queen appeared and produced a beautiful white cow that proceeded to graze on Stapeley Hill, promising the villagers that it would produce sufficient milk for them all, provided that they were not greedy and only brought one acceptable vessel to carry away their share of the milk. However, a wicked witch, Mitchell, schemed to upset the Fairy Queen and at midnight began to milk the cow with a bottomless bucket.

As the witch milked the cow, a terrible storm arose and thunder and lightning illuminated the land, revealing the wasted milk cascading down the hillside. The cow kicked out at the wicked witch and galloped away, never to be seen again, but before Mitchell could escape, the furious Fairy Queen captured her. The following morning there was nothing to be seen of Mitchell except for a solitary stone left on the spot where the Fairy Queen had punished her – the villagers then placed more stones around the spot to stop her escaping.

A persistent claim linked with the caves of the past occurs on Halzer Hill near Church Stretton where from time to time can be heard the screams of a young girl who fell to her death down an old open copper mine shaft.

An interesting old superstition or legend concerns the church at Chirbury where those who walk round the church twelve times on 31 October each year will be given the names of those villagers who will die within the next twelve months. Two men fortified by drink one night in the 18th century decided to put this to the test and as they walked around the graveyard, a voice started to mumble the names of those destined to die within the next twelve months.

Mitchell's stone circle on Stapeley Hill: a single stone surrounded by four others, placed by the villagers to prevent Mitchell's spirit from escaping.

To their horror they heard the name of a friend being called and when they went to warn him, he laughed at their gullibility but within twelve months he was indeed dead! Tradition has it that the dead souls lying in the Chirbury graveyard are unable to find peace unless they warn the living of an impending death.

A story described as folklore but which really appears to be a most brutal and macabre murder story concerns the ancient, tiny village of Worthen. No date is put on the story but it has been told and re-told over the centuries. The Reynolds family living on a small farm were constantly harassed and annoyed by an elderly couple called the Bogles. Finally they had enough and decided to leave the area for a distant farmhouse.

On settling into their new home they discovered that they had left behind an old family heirloom and asked their cowhand Edward to go back and collect it. When Edward returned to their former farm, the Bogles were there and admitted that they had the heirloom but would only part with it if he told them where the Reynolds' new farm was. Edward played along with them and offered to show them but once the heirloom was in his possession, he believed that he could prevent them following him; he was unsuccessful!

The Reynolds were shocked to find the Bogles arriving with Edward and the harassment and annoyance started again. Once again the Reynolds became desperate and hatched a plot. They lit a large fire in the farm and invited the elderly Bogles to sit close by it for warmth. Unbeknown to the Bogles, Edward was hiding beneath a blanket of straw in the corner of the room. He sprang on the unsuspecting pair and threw them into the fire. The Reynolds rushed into the room carrying broomsticks and pitchforks with which they forced the Bogles to remain in the fire until they were consumed!

Shrewsbury has more than 600 recorded incidents of ghostly phenomena and is regarded as one of Britain's most haunted towns. The town has experienced much warfare and violence, and been exposed to the differing cultures of many visitors. It was host to a number of atrocities and the existence of its many fine medieval buildings contain secrets that they sometimes unexpectedly yield to the unsuspecting.

A well-known story concerns the BBC film crew who were using Shrewsbury as the film location for *A Christmas Carol*. Several of the crew were staying at the *Prince Rupert Hotel* on Butcher Row. One night the BBC's Director of Photography, whom one would assume to be reasonably familiar with images, told everyone that he had seen a man in a nightshirt disappear through the hotel wall into a hallway.

The hotel has a reputation for hauntings and he was told of the young man who killed himself in the hotel after his friend went off with his lady. A young lady also hanged herself at the hotel when she was jilted shortly before her marriage. Following complaints from hotel guests over unusual incidents in room number six, the management changed the bedroom and turned it into a staff meeting place! On one occasion a medium was called into the hotel to investigate and claimed to have met the ghost of a young maid who was continually walking up and down the stairs.

At the *Lion Hotel*, Wyle Cop, which winds up the main hill into Shrewsbury, there is also a lively tradition of unexpected guests. A grey lady is often seen on the balcony overlooking the Adam Ballroom and the ghost of a soldier is a frequent visitor to the Tudor Bar.

In 1647 Mrs Foxall of Shrewsbury was burned at the stake for the murder of her husband and for more than two hundred years residents close to the Dingle area where she was executed claimed that her ghost was a regular visitor to the site.

Old Inns are often a good source of ghost stories and the *Dun Cow Inn* near Shrewsbury Abbey has a good story to tell from more modern times. The landlady Mrs Hayes awoke one night in 1980 to see a hooded figure dressed in monk's habit bending over the cot containing her infant daughter. Mrs Hayes distinctly recognised that the figure was unquestionably that of an old monk but strangely, his habit was dotted with bright colours!

The Prince Rupert Hotel on Butcher Row has a reputation for hauntings and supernatural activity.

The ordeal was soon over and the image disappeared but he wasn't done with the family yet. When the infant was around two years old she screamed out in the night telling her anxious parents that a strange man had come into her room. The landlord Mr Hayes and guests have at various times reported seeing apparitions and figures apparently walking through walls.

Ghosts and spirits often return, it is said, because of an injustice which leaves the soul unable to rest in peace. Such is the case in another famous Shrewsbury incident. At the Elizabethan Hall, just outside Shrewsbury, there occurred a fiendish murder when the estate owner Lord Knyvett was brutally murdered by his own son who stabbed him to death. In his death throes, Knyvett stumbled down the stairs to the basement dragging his bleeding body and as he breathed his last, his hand left a bloodied print upon the stone.

The butler was charged with the murder on the evidence of the son and found guilty and sentenced to death. At his trial he said, 'Before heaven I am innocent, although my master's son swears me guilty. And as I perish an innocent man, may those who follow my murdered lord be cursed'. The curse over the years appears to have worked, for no heir to Condover Hall has ever prospered. Even more mysteriously, the bloodied handprint on the stairway defeated all efforts to clean it away. It defied all attempts at chemical-removal and always reappeared, until finally the decision was taken to chip the stone away and eventually the 'bloodied hand' was removed.

Another legacy of a great injustice governs the ghost of Plaish Hall, a grand Elizabethan building with impressive Tudor chimneys located close to Cardington, near Church Stretton.

The owner of the property was Judge William Leighton who was having the house, originally built in stone, rebuilt in brick but wanted the ornate chimneys to be created by a craftsman. It so happened that he had recently tried and sentenced to death just such a craftsman. Seeing his opportunity, he offered to pardon the man in exchange for his expertise in creating the chimneys; his offer was naturally greeted with great relief and the man worked hard to earn his freedom.

However, once the work was completed and the Judge was satisfied with the job, he had the man hanged from one of the chimneys and, it is said, had his body walled up in another of the chimney's cavities.

On stormy winter nights of rain, with the wind whistling down the chimneys of Plaish Hall, it was sometimes said the walls oozed blood and the ghost of the builder could be heard howling from the top of the building. The 'blood' has since been attributed to a combination of rainwater, soot and rusting iron but there is also still the appearance of an old grey lady walking with the figure

Plaish Hall is said to be haunted by the spirits of an old grey lady walking with a male figure and by a man who was brutally hanged from one of the chimneys and hidden in the cavity of another.

of a tall shadowy man to be explained. Is it the builder and his horrified mother? Today the house is once again a private dwelling whose magnificent exterior betrays no hint of its colourful past.

In the nearby churchyard at Cardington is said to be the tomb of the evil judge with an uncomfortable-looking carved figure sitting atop the tomb. However, my best efforts failed to find any evidence of this gravestone.

An entire book has been devoted to ghosts just from Shrewsbury alone but the rest of the county is also rich in stories of the paranormal.

Ludlow Castle is still a magnificent sight and on a clear sunny day exudes all the splendour of its historic past but on a cold, dark winter's night it is a far from hospitable place and occasionally yields a hint of bygone horrors.

Its most famous ghost dates back to the 12th century when the castle was under siege. Helping defend it was Marion de la Bruyere who let her lover, part of the besieging force, into the castle at night by lowering a rope for him to ascend. However, one night instead of ascending the rope alone, he let his men climb up it and into the castle and the siege was over: he had betrayed her.

Marion's revenge was swift. She killed him with his own sword and then jumped from the castle battlements to her death. She is often seen walking near the 'Hanging Tower' and at times noises resembling heavy breathing and gasping are heard. It is not clear whether the noises are hers or those of her lover when he was climbing the rope.

Market Street, Ludlow, is a popular spot with another Ludlow ghost said to be that of a Tudor soldier, Edward Dobson, who died in a fight at the Globe Inn (now the Chang Thai) when he was stationed at Ludlow Castle in 1553. The ghost is bewigged, with a cloak draped around the shoulders, and is seen walking in Market Street and around the spot where he died.

When castles fell into disuse, local people often plundered

the site for stone and wood to enhance their own dwellings. In this way, the ruins became exposed to wind and storm and over the years decay set in and edifices started to crumble. Not far from Ludlow and about a mile from Hopton Heath railway station, are the remains of Hopton Castle that was built around the 12th century. Today the site is Grade 1 listed, on private property and is being secured by English Heritage, as the building requires work to guard against total collapse. The local people, however, did not plunder the castle for its materials, as it was thought to be haunted by the defenceless victims of a brutal, vicious execution in 1644 during the English Civil War.

The Wallop family who were staunch parliamentarians, owned the castle and eventually, as the war progressed, it was surrounded by a Royalist army 500-strong led by Sir Michael Woodhouse. After three weeks of fighting, the defenders eventually negotiated terms with the besiegers; they would lay down their arms and surrender the castle in exchange for their lives. The Royalists, however had no intention of honouring the agreement and they threw Colonel Moore into the prison at Ludlow Castle but as events progressed he was the fortunate one.

The rest of the defenders, 28 men, were tied back-to-back and one by one had their throats cut and their bodies dumped in the moat. It was cold-blooded murder, a merciless execution without honour. A maid was also killed but another maid was allowed to leave as a source of warning to others. Chroniclers claim that two men survived, one hidden in a gap in the castle wall and one, a Major, survived despite a savage beating and being thrown into the moat. Before leaving, the Royalists sacked the castle, weakened the walls and set fire to the structure. The atrocity was later known as the 'Hopton Quarter'.

The local people avoided the site of the murders at Hopton Castle, even more so when tales emerged of ghosts of the massacre and of the four Royalists killed during the siege who were said to roam amongst the ruins. A young lady, the widow of one of the victims, is also said to haunt the ruins crying out for her departed love.

Churchyards are a great favourite for ghost hunters and the church at St Laurence's Ludlow plays host to the ghost of an elderly woman. The tall, grey-haired figure has been seen wandering around the gravestones and has been sighted at the rectory.

An interesting incident in the small village of Stanton Lacy just outside Ludlow occurred in more modern times: 1968 to be precise. A man from Ludlow came to photograph inside St Peter's Church and suddenly, when standing in the chancel, was overcome by terror and left without taking any pictures. He later returned with his wife for company and experienced the same sensation, total fear, and asked to see the vicar the prebendary, L.J. Blashford Snell. This time the three of them entered the church and the vicar witnessed not only the man's terror but also confirmed that his hair was literally standing on end!

The vicar was able to explain that during the Civil War the Cromwellian troops had pursued a young man into the grounds of the church and murdered him there. The 1968 incident was reported in the local and national newspapers. In the chancel arch of the church, there is graffiti carving dated 1649 referring to the young man's murder.

There are two other stories concerning Royalist ghosts still appearing in the lanes of local villages. In the village of Chatwall there are a number of claims of a Royalist trooper riding silently along the roads and similarly, close to Church Stretton at Wilderhope Manor, the ghost of Royalist Major Smalman is allegedly often seen galloping quickly down the narrow lanes adjoining his mansion. During the Civil War he was surrounded at Wilderhope by Roundheads but managed to escape by galloping fiercely through their ranks. Wilderhope Manor, still a magnificent building with its rounded towers overlooking the fields, is believed to be haunted by Major Smalman and a young girl who smiles charmingly at first when seen and then screams horribly.

It was reported that a writer elected to spend a little time at the Manor specifically to investigate the haunting and sightings. After a few days of little activity he climbed the scaffolding to have a look at the plaster ceiling in the main hall and suddenly he was made aware of a tall image standing in the doorway. The figure was wearing a full cloak, a floppy hat with a large plume and thigh-length boots. Not prepared to accept what he had witnessed, he assumed that it was someone in fancy dress and called out from the top of the scaffolding, 'hello'. The figure merely raised its head, glanced in his direction and then walked across the room and straight through the solid wall. He had just seen Major Smalman!

A photographer claims to have captured an incident in the churchyard at Broseley, when a white figure wearing a poke bonnet and carrying a candle was seen by three different people before disappearing.

Another churchyard story involves two fighting monks at St Peter's churchyard, Easthope. From time to time it is claimed that

The graves of two quarrelling monks, both killed during their struggle, lie side by side in the graveyard of St Peter's church at Easthope.

as people walk through the churchyard, the sound of two men fighting are clearly defined. Legend has it that two monks from the Manorhouse quarrelled bitterly, centuries ago, and it developed into a fist-fight culminating in the struggling pair falling down the stairs of the cellar, killing both of them. Side by side in the church-yard at Easthope are two tombs bearing only a simple cross but it seems that the quarrel continues today!

An interesting story revolves around a hunting man, the 'Whipper-In' at Willey Hall in the 18th century, a man called Tom Moody. Hunting was his life and he loved the hounds and the chase of the fox, but he was paranoid about dying, particularly dreading the prospect of somehow being buried alive. He begged his master Lord Forester to respect his wishes before death. He asked to be buried at Barrow, carried by six earth stoppers with his old horse carrying his whip, boots, spurs and cap in the saddle, together with the brush of the last fox killed and a couple of hounds to act as mourners.

He begged that before the coffin lid was sealed, the assembled party would shout three 'halloos' and if he did not respond to that, then he must be dead and the grave could be filled in. Tom Moody did not rise to the call but he has risen since and has been seen several times at the Hall, sometimes accompanied by his favourite hound: the ghost Whipper-In at Willey Hall.

The area around the village of Baschurch has a most macabre presence. An unknown gentleman hanged himself there and on occasions he is seen driving his coach and horses around the area but his sense of direction gives great cause for concern as he is headless! Another headless horseman is said to inhabit the village of Ruyton and is usually seen at midnight when the mist comes up from the valley, enveloping the churchyard and the remains of the old castle. The rider is seen coming through the mist towards the castle keep and then disappears as the mist thickens.

North of Wem along the B5476 there is a tiny hamlet off the main road reached by a very careful journey down extremely narrow country lanes, passable by only one vehicle at a time. At a tiny break in the road can be seen the large impressive but rusting iron gates of a substantial, private property, barely visible through the surrounding trees and hedgerows. The house is the subject of a curious tale that must have had some sort of foundation to warrant the action taken.

The story involves the small settlement at Coton in which Coton Hall, belonging to Corbet Kynaston, was said to be haunted by him following his death. In 1788 the local vicar David Evans decided that complaints from tenants about the noise and activity, from the ghost of old Corbet was proving to be too much and required controlling.

Together with several other clerics, he attended the Hall and during a candlelit vigil they prayed for the peace of the soul of the departed. Around midnight they enticed Corbet's spirit to enter into a bottle that was immediately sealed and thrown into a nearby pond. This remedy was supposed to be effective for one thousand years but just ten years later tenants complained that milk churns had been rolled about and for no apparent reason a bush around the edge of the pond had burst into flames. Old Corbet was not going without a fight! Not far from Wem and close by Shawbury, a trip down a minor road reveals the remains of a once-superb castle dating back to the 13th century.

Moreton Corbet Castle is now reduced to a shell but it quite clearly indicates that it was once a formidable fortress and later additions in the 16th century were made in the Roman style. The Corbets acquired the castle through marriage in 1239 and successive generations added to the building but the prime mover was Robert Corbet, a favourite of Elizabeth I who started an ambitious building programme around the late 1500s but he died in 1583 before it was completed. His brothers elected to continue the work and in particular Sir Vincent Corbet, who became the unwitting victim of this ghost story.

At the time of King James I, the Puritans were being persecuted and a neighbour of Sir Vincent's, Paul Holmyard, was being victimised. Sir Vincent in a kindly act gave him sanctuary in the house. However the man's fanatical beliefs became an embarrassment and a nuisance and eventually Sir Vincent was forced to ban him from Moreton Corbet Castle.

For a time Holmyard lived rough in the woods, barely surviving but one day he emerged to confront Sir Vincent and placed a curse on him and his family. He told him that, despite his riches, none of his bloodline would ever live in the house. The prophesy was fulfilled when Sir Vincent and his son Andrew both died without ever moving to live in the renovated, restructured building. Andrew's widow moved into the Castle in 1638 and for many years afterwards it was said that the gaunt, bedraggled figure of Paul Holmyard could be seen walking through the ruins as if he were making sure that no re-building work was taking place.

The remains of Moreton Corbet Castle, cursed and now haunted by the figure of Paul Holmyard.

A well-known ghost story well worth the retelling occurred following a Christmas Eve party at an old-timber framed house just outside Minsterley. With the party in full swing, the host poured his guests generous amounts of after-dinner port and as they were well into the celebrations, the jollity and well-being was shattered by an unearthly whistling from somewhere outside. The sound was so evil that it unnerved the guests to such an extent that they scrambled in panic for the door.

When they all gathered safely together outside it was observed that the host was missing but only one man was brave enough to re-enter the house to search for him. What he found has gone down in the annals of ghost hunting as the 'Devil's Talon': the horrified guest found the body of the host lying under a table, his bloodied body, clothes and the fixtures all around the scene shredded by what was described as a giant claw; the Devil's Talon.

Unrequited love is often the reason for the tragic wandering in perpetuity of the soul and such a tale is that of the White Lady of Longnor. Sometimes at the Villa close by Black Pool, parties would spot an unexpected guest joining in the dancing and the gaiety. So real was the vision that one young man is said to have fallen in love with her, dressed as she was in a white wedding gown. However when he reached out to grasp her she just slipped away and then vanished in front of the astonished partygoers. Broken-hearted, she had drowned herself some years before in the Black Pool when her fiancé deserted her. No more dancing parties are held at the Villa and the Black Pool has long since been filled in.

Ghost stories set at night on lonely roads are always a favourite and a particularly fascinating incident from the 20th century occurred one night when a Mr Owen from Little Severn Hall was driving home along the Broseley Road from Bridgnorth and through the village of Astley Abbots. Not far from his destination by a lay-by near Boldings, he spotted a young woman about five feet tall wearing dark clothes, a long skirt to the ground and a

185

shawl wrapped around her head. As he drew closer in the car she suddenly, to his astonishment, disappeared.

The next day he related his experience to his boss who told him the local facts. The young lady was Hannah Philips who had lived on the other side of the river and was due to be married at Astley Abbots church. A couple of days before the wedding day she visited the church to help with the arrangements but tragically on her way back home she slipped and fell into the river and drowned. She was never seen again in the flesh but from time to time she is now spotted on the road to the church, preparing for the big day that is still to happen!

A couple had the courage to report another road story of an incident that occurred in 2005. They were driving along a small road between Shropshire's Bomere Heath and Walford and were close to the railway bridge when all of a sudden they saw an elderly lady dressed in grey and wearing a headscarf run across the road just ahead of them. Nothing unusual in that, you might think but they reported that the figure looked wispy and unreal and her clothes moved slower than her body. Even more bizarrely, the driver reported that as far as he was concerned, she had crossed the road from the left hand side but his wife was adamant that the figure had crossed from the right hand side!

In the 1970s a motorcyclist riding on the road between Ash Magna and Ash Grange reported seeing the ghostly figure of a monk, his face covered by a hood but, incredibly, the figure was floating about 30 centimetres off the ground. In the late 1960s on the A41 between Chetwynd Aston and Chetwynd Hall, a lady, Madam Pigott who had died in childbirth, was seen many times carrying her baby and sometimes combing its hair. Eventually twelve parsons were brought in to exorcise and bring peace to her tormented soul but despite that, in 1969, two motorists on separate occasions claimed to have seen a figure in white walking along the road near the church.

The remnants of Acton Burnell Castle, a once magnificent building, now haunted by a mysterious young girl dressed in white lace.

The small community of Acton Burnell has two incidents worthy of reporting, both involving young ladies. At Acton Burnell Castle in 2004 a girl with a ghostly appearance dressed in white lace was seen and photographed by a young female student. The image when revealed was blurred, almost misty, but looked like a face. The student also reported hearing scratching noises from the ruined site.

At Acton Burnell House a spirit made one decisive appearance and has not been seen since. The figure walked into a bedroom and announced, 'Mass is at eight o'clock,' before disappearing. She was not a member of staff and whoever or whatever she was, her appearance is still a mystery.

A very sad incident underlining the bond between mothers and children that may exist in the afterlife, if there is such a thing, occurred at a 16th century site now known as the Magpie House Restaurant at the foot of Bridgnorth's Cartway.

The two children of the house were playing in the cellar when somehow they became locked in. No one knew they were

187

there. They were trapped underground as the nearby River Severn started to rise in high flood, burst its banks and flooded the properties by the riverside. The children locked in the cellar had no way of escape and were drowned. The distraught parents had marble statues made of their children that are still there today in the Terrace Gardens. The building also displays a plaque testifying to the mother's undying love for her children. However, her soul is still in denial and the Black Lady, as she is called, has been seen on many occasions moving around the building and often she can be heard softly crying or laughing, perhaps remembering happier times, although her soul is still clearly restless and unable to cope with the guilt of the accidental death of her children.

The River Severn also features in another tragic incident involving children. Two young twins from Ferry Road, Jackfield, near Ironbridge, were happily playing on the spoil heaps left behind from the workings of the Dunnill Tile Works. Over the past few winter days the Severn had risen and its waters had started to erode the surrounding areas. As the children played on the bank, it suddenly collapsed, throwing them into the river.

The swollen waters carried the boys down to just below the footbridge at Jackfield where their bodies were caught up in overhanging tree branches. When the bodies were recovered they were still holding hands. Even today it is said that the house where the bodies were brought is filled from time to time with the sound of children crying.

There is also another ghost story concerning the village of Jackfield, alleged to have taken place at the *Boat Inn*. One December night the locals were in the pub playing cards with a stranger when someone picking up a fallen card noticed that the stranger had a club-foot. No sooner had he made this discovery than a great gust of wind hit the building, swept into the room, and the man vanished: the locals were convinced that they had played cards with the devil.

The footbridge at Jackfield where the bodies of two young boys were found holding hands after being swept into the swollen river and drowned.

In more recent times, the landlady of the *Boat Inn* claims that she woke up one night to find a young girl standing by her bedside. The image was very real, so much so that when the young girl beckoned to her, she followed her downstairs. To her surprise she found that a ground floor window had been forced open, but no one had ventured inside.

The Boat Inn is very close to the banks of the River Severn and the pub building has on the front wall of the property a list of the highest levels recorded by the River Severn overflowing its banks. Perhaps the young girl had joined the ranks of many Shropshire people who have drowned in this powerful river.

The village of Ratlinghope has a most peculiar legend handed down over the centuries and concerns what can only be described as a spectral spectacle. It has been described as the Phantom Funeral and usually occurs in twilight in the early morning mist.

Two horses wearing black plumes pull a polished, decorated carriage accompanied by pall-bearers wearing long coats and top hats. The cortege's route is always the same: it moves down the narrow lane past Ratlinghope church and up out of the hill on the other side of the village and away.

No one knows whose funeral it is or where it is going. But over the centuries villagers claim that this cortege has been seen from time to time.

Shropshire's industrial heritage is built alongside or over many medieval or older sites.

The old Buildwas Power Station, formerly Ironbridge Power Station, was partly built on the site of an old abbey, which unsurprisingly disgruntled the previous occupants, disturbing their rest these past few centuries. Workers at the power station reported seeing the ghostly figure of a monk walking through the modern building and another employee claimed to have seen a woman floating in front his eyes before disappearing. The nearby village of Leighton has reported further visual and audible paranormal experiences connected, perhaps, with the old abbey.

In Bridgnorth there is an old carpet factory with a regular visitor, 'Old Mo'. When the last member of staff was about to leave one night, she encountered a figure as she walked through the old part of the building. Very clearly she recognised that the figure, dressed in a white habit, was the ghost of a monk known as 'Old Mo'.

He walked slowly towards her, up the factory steps, but when he reached the top, just short of her, he turned and went down again. The factory is no longer active and it seems that the spirits may be at rest. However, recent housing developments on the site have unearthed parts of an old friary and this may well trigger the ghosts of the past to take further action!

The *Tontine Hotel*, Ironbridge, has its own ghost who has frequented the hotel, particularly room five, since the 1950s.

Frank Griffin was a resident at the hotel during part of the 1950s but also was a tenant at a house in Ketley. After murdering his landlady in Ketley, he returned to *The Tontine Hotel* but very soon the police linked him to the murder and he was arrested. He was tried, convicted and hanged for his crime in Shrewsbury. His ghost has been seen at the hotel on several occasions and so has the ghost of a young girl whose origin is unknown. The staff and guests have reported lights going on and off without contact, taps switched on by themselves and bottles moving of their own accord!

Madeley Court House is an old Elizabethan building full of character, once close to the site of a row of old miner's cottages,

The Tontine Hotel at Ironbridge has been haunted by resident ghost Frank Griffin since his death by hanging in the 1950s.

long since demolished. However, some of the previous occupants of the cottages make appearances from time to time. An old lady is a frequent visitor to Madeley Court and monks have also been seen walking in the grounds. On one memorable, but probably frightening, occasion a family claimed to have seen several monks sitting on the cross beams in the Great Hall!

Workers at a limestone pit at Benthall Edge around the 1890s were robbed of their wages when a man carrying the mining crews week's wages was attacked, robbed and murdered. The robbers tied and bound the man before throwing him into a pit and then covering the site with a huge heavy stone. The man was buried alive and although he struggled and yelled, the noise from his workmates drowned out his cries. When eventually his body was found he had been crushed to death by the weight of the stone. For many years afterwards it was said that the terrified man's spirit could be heard screaming from the grave.

A more modern incident has manifested itself at the Cosford Aerospace Museum at Albrighton. The museum is the proud resting place of the last Avro Lincoln Bomber and is said to be haunted by a pilot who has been seen in the cockpit. Investigators left overnight-recording equipment which amazingly, despite the fact that there was no activity at all in the hangar area or indeed in the museum, played back to them the following day all the busy sounds and noises of an active airport.

The village of Much Wenlock was featured in the newspapers and on BBC Midland television in 2002 following the ghostly happenings resulting from the building excavations required for improvements at the Spar shop supermarket just off The Square. The builders disturbed old ground underneath the building, bringing up bits of old pottery and several human bones. Staff at that time started to experience weird happenings: trolleys moved on their own, heavy breathing was apparent to a number of staff, others felt as if they had been touched by unseen hands but there was nobody ever there and one lady saw an apparition for about 15 seconds as she entered a room to wash cups. The excavations were taking place on the site of the 12th century abbey cemetery.

Much Wenlock is also known for the ghostly manifestations at the Raynald's House which was built in 1682. This fine old building appears still to play host to Victorian children whose faces have been seen peering from the windows and playing with spinning tops on the balcony.

Chapter Eight

DISASTERS, ACCIDENTS AND TRAGEDIES

The scarred landscape of Shropshire bears testimony to the way in which Man has sought to exploit and change the earth's resources available to him over thousands of years. Many regions of the county are pitted with Man's attempts to extract Shropshire's valuable minerals and the countryside has been carved out to build the Shropshire canal system and then shortly afterwards, great tracts of the county were fashioned to accommodate the railway system.

There is evidence of copper mining during the Bronze Age around the Llanymynech area. The Romans, 2000 years ago, were extensively mining lead. Vital minerals were available locally to those industrious, skilful and brave enough to risk their lives in the pits or shafts deep below the surface.

The Clee Hill area is a prime example of man's early efforts to extract coal and iron ore, especially around the 1700s. Shallow shafts or pits were dug by hand, linked by adjoining short passages, but as the pits got deeper there was a real risk of collapse and failure of ventilation. Instinct told the men when a pit was at its optimum depth and another would be dug close by and the process started over again. The actual shafts are called 'bell pits' and the raised feature at the surface is called 'bell-pitting', a distinctive sight in the Clee Hill area. At other times, mines consisted mainly of long tunnels bored into the side of a hill to get at the coal seam.

At one time Shropshire had an extensive mining industry. Coal was mined mainly at Oswestry, Shrewsbury, Coalbrookdale, Wyre Forest and the Clee Hills. Lead was mined at Llanymynech and in south west Shropshire; copper at Clive, Weston, Eardiston and Harmer Hill; limestone at Lilleshall; and stone was quarried in various parts of the county.

The work was exceedingly dangerous although safety improvements were made from time to time. Steam engines were introduced to pump water out of the shafts in the 18th century, but a second, escape shaft was only made a legal requirement by the end of the 19th century, and men for a time used canaries as an indicator of the levels of toxic gases in the shafts of the coal mines. Their bright yellow colour made them more easily seen in the dark depths and their susceptibility to the quality of the air gave the miners an early indication of danger.

Nevertheless, there were very many life-threatening scenarios in those early pits affecting all mining industries. Roof collapse, flooding, gas, fire, equipment failure, suffocation and even falling down open mine shafts often claimed the lives of the miners while the damp conditions and coal dust would have a detrimental effect on the health of those who survived into retirement.

The men would often travel great distances to reach a working mine, often setting off in the early hours even in the depths of icy winters and then would work in cramped conditions in a freezing environment, wearing rough, hand-made clothes, in an attempt to give some kind of protection from the elements. It was even a practice that some Shropshire men would fashion their own type of early safety helmet by treating an old bowler hat with resin or other stiffening products in order to make it more resilient to rock falls. However, nothing would afford protection against a total roof collapse.

As the lead and coal industries thrived, so did the communities around the mines and for a time between 1850-75 Shropshire provided Britain with much of its lead. The country was prosperous with more than 200 mines flourishing!

Mercifully the mining history of Shropshire, despite its intensity, has had relatively few real disasters compared to other parts of the country where hundreds of miners have been killed in single tragedies. Even so, mining is a very dangerous occupation and deaths were a daily occurrence.

One of the earliest recorded fatalities occurred at the Meadow Pit mine at Blists Hill on 2 January 1810. An underground fire swept through the passages of the mine but luckily all 13 men and the pit ponies escaped unharmed. However, the following day a party of four went down into the mine to assess the prospects of returning to work. During their inspection the four men were overcome from the carbon monoxide and all perished, leaving between them 19 orphaned children.

In 1858 at the Pitchcroft limestone mine, Lilleshall Hill, three men working underground were crushed to death when a huge stone slab dislodged from overhead and fell on them as they worked below. In the same pit in 1860 an underground flood submerged the shafts, drowning all the pit ponies.

One of the worst mining disasters to affect the county occurred in 1864 at the Brick Kiln Leasow pit near Madeley. Chain loops were used to raise and lower men into the long deep shaft and on this occasion, as nine men were ascending, the chains became unhooked and all nine plunged to their deaths at the bottom of the pit. The whole community of Madeley was devastated by the disaster. Victims Edward Wallett left four children and John Tranter left five children, two of the dead were under 18 and four, including a boy of twelve, were under 16.

The victims were all buried at St Michael's Church in Madeley in a communal grave with an iron top and an iron enclosure. Madeley Wood Company who owned the mine ordered all their works to close early on the day of the funeral, which was attended by 2,500 miners and colliery workers as well as their families.

The grave has recently received a grant from the Heritage Lottery Fund and the Madeley Living History Project has presided over the restoration of the site. Today Madeley is a thriving, populous part of Telford with its mining history gone but not forgotten.

The use of the chain system could at times prove lethal if proper maintenance was not carried out and deterioration had set in. In 1872, at the Springwell Pit, Dawley, there was no cage for the men to ascend and descend, and chains were the access method. Eight miners were riding the chain when it suddenly snapped and all eight fell to their deaths.

Gas once again proved to be a lethal danger when in 1875, at the Lodgebank Colliery, Donnington Wood, an underground fire triggered off toxic gases suffocating to death 11 men and a horse; the mine was later christened the 'Slaughter Pit'.

A horrific accident occurred in 1895 and is referred to as the 'Snailbeach Mining Disaster'. It was 6 March and the approach of spring seemed far away as a bitterly cold winter continued. Records at the time report heavy snow, frequent gales and severe frosts that had hung around for weeks, making conditions underground even harder. Adding to the strife, the men had to battle their way through the awful weather conditions from the surrounding villages in order to get to the lead mine for the first shift of the day, by 6am!

Stripping off their day-wear, they would don their working clothes, old jackets, rough home-made shirts and thick, often moleskin, trousers. Home-made re-enforced hats had a soft lining with a piece of clay stuck on the front to hold a candle.

It seems absolutely unbelievable that human beings could descend perhaps 1,700 feet into the dark bowels of the earth with just a lit candle to direct them! Snailbeach Mine, whose shaft went down 750 feet, operated a cage system using the double pulley principle so that as one cage descended, the other ascended. A steel rope was fixed to the top from which the cage was suspended and it was controlled from an engine house.

Left:
The memorial for the nine men killed during the horrific mining disaster at the Brick Kiln Leasow pit, Madeley in 1864.

Right:
The nine victims are buried in a communal grave in St Michael's churchyard. The grave has been recently restored by the Madeley Living History Project.

One shift had already descended that morning and as they waited at the bottom for the rest of their colleagues to join them before going about their allocated duties, they had no indication of the horror that was about to be enacted.

At the top of the shaft, as the seven men were about to enter the cage for the descent, one of the miners, George Lewis, told his son that they needed the drills which had been taken to the blacksmith's shop for sharpening the day before. Will Lewis offered to go back to the cabin and get them: that decision saved his life.

In his absence, his colleagues decided to descend and George Williams, the engine driver, started to lower the cage. Suddenly the steel rope snapped and the cage fell like a stone more than 250 yards to the bottom of the shaft.

The men waiting at the bottom in a side room rushed to see if they could help, after the impact which shook the ground all around them had subsided. The rescuers were shocked and sickened by what they saw. The steel cage 7ft 6in high, had been crushed to no more than 18 inches and the mangled bodies inside had been reduced to pulp. It was a spectacle that the toughened miners would never get out of their minds.

Young Will Lewis returned to the shaft just in time to see the steel rope whipping high overhead towards the engine room where George Williams narrowly missed decapitation by the lethal recoil of the steel hawser!

The men of the earlier shift had a miraculous escape, and climbed out of the pit using the ladder road by the nearby pumping shaft.

The dead men, all from nearby Snailbeach, Perkin's Beach, Pennerley, Minsterley, Stiperstones, Wagbeach and Gorsty Bank, reflected the tight-knit community of mining. The rewards of their profession had to be balanced by the dangers that were ever-present. The inquest formally recorded that the breaking of a defective rope caused the deaths at Snailbeach Lead Mine.

The old mine shaft at Snailbeach, where six men lost their lives after the steel rope lowering their cage into the mine snapped, causing the cage to plummet to the bottom of the 750ft shaft.

A tragic consequence was the death of Anne Blower who was incorrectly informed that her husband had died in the accident. On hearing this news she collapsed and died the following day.

On Tuesday 26 April 1904 Granville Colliery suffered a tragedy when a party of men were working in the middle of the night at 3.30am. The task was to introduce a new wooden pump that had to be lowered down the mine-shaft; the rod was 46 feet long and 13 inches square with a weight of around 25 tons! It was attached to a rope with an inch-thick chain fastened once around the rod 13 feet from the end.

Three men were positioned in the cage a short way down the mineshaft acting as guide to the object as it was slowly lowered through the top of the pit. Suddenly the weight of the rod caused it to slip through the bindings and it hurtled down the mineshaft carrying the cage and its hapless occupants with it, who all died.

The mine was meanwhile unable to pump water and it was quickly realised that the rising water levels had isolated 19 horses in a separate part of the mine. Some of the men tried to get to the horses using rafts to navigate the five feet or so deep water.

After more than four days, men wading up to their armpits through the water were able to bring the trapped horses some sustenance. However after fitting a new pump rod, further problems developed and once again the waters cut off the horses' food supplies. It was almost ten days before they were once again fed by which time four were known to have died. The horses' ordeal meant that from 25 April when the crisis first erupted until 17 May, they were fed only once!

Chain and rope malfunction led to yet another disaster on 4 December 1910 at the Kemberton Pit, near Madeley, owned by the Madeley Wood Colliery Company.

On the Sunday night fireman George Gough was waiting to descend to carry out night repairs in preparation for the first shift of Monday morning when 200-300 men would be descending into the mine. Only nine men turned up to do the repairs, so Gough ordered two of these men to stay behind and wait for the others. This order saved two lives. The cage with seven men aboard had descended no more than 40 yards when the rope snapped and it plummeted more than 800 feet to the ground! By the time the rescuers got there, all that was visible was a tangled mass of blood and flesh.

Somehow they got the body parts to the surface where they were placed in the engine room for formal identification by their grief-stricken families. Five men and two boys had been crushed and 16 children were orphaned. The inquest heard that the rope had been checked on the morning of the fatality and was believed to be fine and it was also revealed that it was capable of a breaking point at 60 tons whereas the total of the cage and the seven occupants had only amounted to 30 cwt; why it had failed remained a mystery.

201

All the mines, shops and schools closed on the day of the funeral, all houses drew their curtains and the whole town of Madeley joined in the mourning; the community pulled together and a collection was made for the widows and orphans.

The harsh conditions and the hardships forged camaraderie between the men working underground and each was aware that their lives depended on the reliability and good sense of their workmates. It was not an environment for laxity: one break in concentration or piece of tomfoolery could cost lives.

At an incident at the Woodhouse Colliery, Priorslee, in 1916, there was a winding mishap in which five men were badly injured. In a totally selfless act, local doctor Justin McCarthy volunteered to go to their aid and he was lowered down the mineshaft by sling. His prompt and brave action ensured that they received very early attention and were spared more serious consequences.

As well as the incidents already recounted, there were frequent accidents where miners, visitors and children fell into open mine shafts to their deaths.

One such account, slightly different but nevertheless interesting, was recorded in the Annual Register in 1759 referring to an incident on Clee Hill.

The story concerns a foxhunt that took place in the region of Clee Hill near Ludlow, close by a number of open coal pits. It was said to be an area requiring caution and was hardly suitable for horse, rider, hounds and fox! The huntsmen sensibly held back as the chase continued over the more dangerous terrain until suddenly the fox threw itself into an open pit. Twelve hounds followed him in and five died on the spot and several others were badly hurt! The account doesn't tell us whether the fox got away but it does mention that several miners were working in the 200ft deep pit at the very moment when the unexpected visitors dropped in on them!

Human nature being what it is, there is always someone prepared to take advantage of others' misfortune or to play on the sympathies and good nature of people being prepared to respond to those less fortunate than themselves.

During the 19th century, as seasonal work finished in the Shropshire area, some of the local women would travel to London to find work around autumn time. Many of these girls were 'pit' girls looking to earn some money either in the market garden stalls or in the fields.

In October 1839 the *Salopian Journal* published a story of what we would today call a scam, in which a gang from Shropshire had been knocking on doors in the London area purporting to be collecting money for the widows and orphans of a mining disaster in Shropshire.

The woman, Mary Jones, using also the name Rigby, was arrested with her teenage daughter after being observed calling at the homes and presenting the occupants with printed sheets of paper. The prosecutor told the hearing that the gang comprised 14 in number, all well-known to the authorities, who had practised their particular fraud for some time. Both Jones and her husband had served time in the House of Correction and they were once again charged with the same offence.

Mary Jones was evasive and uncooperative and was sentenced once again to hard labour in the House of Correction. Her particular fraud was distasteful because she and her gang were using other people's very real hardship as their own to squeeze money from people touched by their harrowing tales.

The printed paper handed to house-owners to elicit donations from them was printed in full in the *Salopian Journal*. It said:

'I do hereby certify that the bearers here of my employment in the coal mines in the parish of Hadley Old-Fields, in Shropshire, when a most melancholy accident of fire-damp took place in the pits in which the unfortunate sufferers were at work; 25 men, 14 boys and 16 horses were burnt to death, and nine more dreadfully injured, leaving their friends, ten widows, and 36 children to

bewail their loss. The accident has caused the works to be stopped
and reduced the bearers to a state of misery, and almost starvation.
Not less than 450 were thrown out of employment by the above
melancholy event. We hope therefore that our sufferings will plead
for us and that these facts will move your hearts to enable you to
assist us in our present time of need. Gentlemen, their characters
are unimpeachable for sobriety, industry and honesty. They have
worked for me many years and gave me every satisfaction. They
will honestly account to their fellow sufferers for every trifle they
may be intrusted [sic] with by a generous public who know that
fire is obtained at the hazard of the lives of their fellow creatures.'
Signed: Rev. C. Clayton, Mr. H. Lawley, Mr. B. Rowley,
J. Onion, Master of the works.
For its time, quite ingenious!

Railway accidents

The coming of the railway changed the face of Shropshire, bringing
huge improvements in mobility, enhancing the cultures of social
migration and trade. Families and friends were brought closer
together and not only did the coming of the railways generate in
itself massive employment opportunities but trade was enhanced
by the more fluid movement of goods, irrespective of size.

The canal companies quickly realised in the early 1800s
that the railway would soon render the canal system as a mode of
transport virtually obsolete and they started to convert themselves
into railway companies.

In 1846, the Shropshire Union Railway & Canal Company
became an amalgamated consortium of the former canal companies,
Chester, Ellesmere, Birmingham/Liverpool and Shrewsbury,

vowing to establish 155 miles of railway by converting old canal routes and carving out new routes. Eventually more than 2,000 miles of old canal routes would be given over to railway lines throughout the country.

More amalgamations were to follow before the first railway line Stafford to Shrewsbury was launched in 1849.

The first recorded fatalities occurred during the construction of two magnificent iron Victorian 101-foot arch spans, which sat upon stone abutments erected over the River Severn at Preston Boats, (today Belvedere Bridge) about two miles short of Shrewsbury on the Stafford/Shrewsbury line. Two workers fell off the span and drowned in the river below and shortly afterwards, while digging the cutting close to Abbey Foregate near Shrewsbury, the whole bank collapsed trapping one of the men who was suffocated before rescuers were able to reach him.

Considering the dangers and the lack of today's modern technical safety measures, fatalities were low, but when they did occur they were inevitably caused by human error. In July 1852 a passenger engine, *The Mazeppa*, was docked in the sheds at Abbey Foregate to have a leaky valve repaired. The engineer completed the repair in good time and left his shift a few minutes earlier, leaving a gap before the replacement arrived.

When the new shift turned up, the engine was gone! The departing engineer had left the engine in gear and as the steam pressure built up following the repair of the leaky valve, the engine slowly started to move of its own accord. A horrified worker watched it go past him and, noticing no human presence in the cab, raised the alarm.

Another train set off in pursuit but before any intervention could take place, *The Mazeppa* had entered Donnington station and had run into the back of the 6am from Shrewsbury waiting to pull out of the station. It was fortunate that only one passenger was killed.

Another human error proved to be very costly when the driver of a train was killed in January 1858 at Priors Lee. Robert Munslow was driving a locomotive laden with coal for the furnaces at Priors Lee when he had to pull up at a level crossing. The gatekeeper had gone to lunch so he stepped out of the cab to open the gates. As he moved in front of the train, it ran over him, crushing him to death. He had left the engine in gear but had not applied the brake properly!

A lack of system caused the death of a driver in October 1875 in the railyard at Potts Yard, Abbey Foregate. An *LNWR* goods train had been shunting in the yard when it pushed three wagons that somehow had crossed over the safety blocks and started to run down the incline towards the Llanymynech line. The horrified driver of a train pulling fourteen wagons laden with minerals coming up the hill towards Abbey Foregate Road Bridge, saw the runaway wagons heading straight for him down the incline. All he could do was apply his brakes and wait for the moment of impact.

The trains collided and the engine and the first six wagons were hurled off the track but sadly the driver was crushed between the bunker and the firebox.

However the worst railway disaster to affect Shropshire occurred in Shrewsbury in 1907. On the night of 15 October the Salop Infirmary was filled to just under capacity with 102 beds occupied, compared to the hospital's full complement of 120 beds but as the night sister settled down with everything seemingly in order, at 2.25am came the call that she would remember all her life. There had been a major rail crash at Shrewsbury Railway station and the survivors were being ferried urgently to Salop Infirmary.

A mail train had inexplicably come hurtling into Shrewsbury station, a massive missile weighing 400 tons travelling at 60 miles per hour. After a horrendous screeching of brakes it had derailed itself in a mass of crushed metal and escaping steam. For a time a hushed silence descended and then from all sides local people rushed to the site to give whatever help they could as the emergency services rallied to help the injured and the dying.

Back at Salop Infirmary, the night sister woke Miss Clack, the Acting Matron and told her that a fleet of vehicles were heading for the hospital with emergency cases. Extra staff were called in and very quickly the operating theatre was prepared, beds were allocated and the two accident wards, located conveniently close to the operating theatre, were primed for action.

The doors burst open to reveal the first of the patients and as the night progressed the doctors and nurses were commended for their efficiency. Wet clothes were stripped from the patients and a 'Bovril' nurse provided hot drinks for those suffering from cold and from shock while staff with a dressing wagon moved from bed to bed applying stitches to open wounds and securing fractured bones.

At 5am in the morning more staff turned up in answer to the emergency call and incredibly, by 7am, everything was spick and span, despite the fact that 29 accident victims had been admitted to the hospital and 41 others had received treatment before going home.

The long night for the Matron and her team was made even more complicated by the rush to the hospital by the media radio and newspapers anxious to be the first to find out the detail.

It was Shrewsbury's worst-ever railway accident, with 18 deaths: three postal workers, four railway staff including the driver and fireman, and eleven passengers, all from Shrewsbury. Although many passengers survived, some had severe injuries.

Reaction was swift and there was an enquiry the day after the crash at *The Raven Hotel* chaired by Colonel Yorke. The Board of Trade delegate was a certain Mr David Lloyd George who would one day become one of the country's most renowned Prime Ministers.

The enquiry, lacking real evidence, concluded that the driver may have fallen asleep and awoken too late, hence the slamming on of the brakes and the subsequent derailing. It was revealed that the train had left Crewe station eight minutes late and had clearly been trying to make up for lost time. The weather was normal and no faults had been revealed to do with the train's braking system but there was a suggestion that the locomotive had insufficient braking power and this would be an area given greater attention in later designs.

The Shrewsbury Sorting Office raised a memorial plaque to the memory of their staff who had died in the accident.

During this time Tom Owen, the father of Wilfred Owen, was the stationmaster at Shrewsbury and in January 1908 he organised a staff social and dinner in order to raise morale.

In October 2007, to commemorate the 100th anniversary of the accident, there was a memorial service held at Shrewsbury Abbey.

Chapter Nine

THE BATTLE OF SHREWSBURY JULY 1403

Shropshire has had more than its share of violence, war, fights and skirmishes over the last 1,600 years, but there has been only one major battle on Shropshire soil and very violent and bloody it was.

At the height of the summer, July 1403, thousands of men armed to the teeth with longbows, swords, daggers, spiked poles, axes, spears and clubs wended their way through the villages of Shropshire. The rebel army passed south through Whitchurch, having paused in Cheshire, a stronghold for their cause, to gather a contingent of the much-feared and much-respected Cheshire Archers, before making their way down to Shrewsbury. The opposing army loyal to King Henry IV, which had been assembled for a different purpose, was heading north to fight, as he thought, alongside the Northumberland Percy's against the Scots and had reached Nottingham, but on hearing of the rebellion it immediately diverted and headed west towards Shrewsbury.

The King's army crossed the River Severn at Atcham and

was the first to arrive in Shrewsbury. When the rebels arrived at the outskirts of the town and saw to their horror that the King's banners were flying over Shrewsbury, they diverted to Berwick in Shropshire to regroup. Later that day King Henry crossed the Severn at Uffington and spent the night in contemplation at Haughmond Abbey.

The leaders, the protagonists on both sides, knew each other well and at one time had been close friends and allies.

When Henry IV forcibly removed Richard II from the throne in 1399 and indeed murdered him, he was at the time supported by the powerful Percy family led by Sir Henry Percy, better known as Hotspur. But over time the Percys had become disillusioned with Henry's rule. Supported by his father the Earl of Northumberland and expecting support from the Welsh Prince Owain Glyndwr, Hotspur in July 1403 had decided that the time was right to finally depose the King and he switched sides; he was also supported by the Earl of Worcester and Earl of Douglas from Scotland, as well as various knights from Shropshire and Lancashire and by many troops from the Chester region. The rebel army wore the late Richard II's white hart emblem as they passed through the villages.

The King was supported by his son Henry, Prince of Wales, who would later inherit the throne as King Henry V, as well as by many experienced veterans of warfare such as the Earl of Dunbar.

Estimates vary as to the number of men assembled at Shrewsbury, as numerical accuracy wasn't a science and on the medieval battlefield nobody actually enforced a roll call! So in the 1992 edition of *The Battle Book*, Bryan Perrett suggests that Henry's army was about 14,000 strong and the rebels numbered around 10,000; whereas historian Stephen Maxfield in *The Battle of Shrewsbury* has the armies at 6,000 or 7,000 on each side.

The following morning, 21 July, Henry began moving his army from the Haughmond area in an attempt to cut off Hotspur's withdrawal. The two armies probably faced one another around

Harlescott, each side mindful of the range of the deadly longbow.

The monks from Haughmond Abbey and Shrewsbury Abbey tried to mediate between the factions and for a time it seemed that battle could be averted, particularly when Henry offered generous settlement terms.

However, Hotspur prevaricated to such an extent that Henry realised that he was stalling, waiting for imminent re-inforcements from the north in his father the Earl of Northumberland and from Wales, from Owain Glyndwr. The King also realised that very little remained of the day, so with sunset merely a couple of hours away, he ordered the first wave of attacks to go in.

Most good battle stories carry a legend and Shrewsbury is no different. The night before the battle, whilst camped three miles away at Berwick, Hotspur remembered that he had been told in the past by a fortune teller that he would die at Berwick, though he had believed at the time that it referred to Berwick in Northumberland. The final omen occurred when Hotspur called for his favourite sword, used by him in many a battle, only to be told that it had been left behind in Berwick: chroniclers claim that when he realised the significance of both events, he turned pale.

Reports of the battle indicate that the first attack launched by the royal army was through a field of peas and that the King's army was repulsed by the deadly response of the rebel Cheshire archers and their longbows. Soon the field echoed to the cries of the wounded and the ground was littered with the dead and the dying. The sky was said to rain with falling arrows as over 3,000 archers let fly an arrow on average every six seconds; it was a maelstrom of death descending from the skies.

The King's men fell back in disarray and Hotspur led the charge down the hill after them. Hand-to-hand fighting at its deadliest ensued, face-to-face hacking, stabbing, thrusting, impaling – brutal, unforgiving and relentless.

Two things turned the battle in King Henry's favour. The

first occurred when his son, young Prince Henry, led a counter-attack at the rear of the rebel army and then as dusk descended, Hotspur was killed. The rebels lost heart and started to disintegrate and flee. However, no mercy was offered and the retreating rebels were pursued for several miles as the slaughter continued.

The following morning, Sunday 22 July 1403, the carnage in the cold light of day was horrific: battered, mangled bodies lay scattered around over several miles. Arrows protruding from many bodies were stuck upright in the ground like some dreadful crop, 'a crop of death'.

Chroniclers recorded that there had never been so many casualties in such a short engagement. Records indicate that the King's army, despite victory, had suffered the greater number of casualties, probably sustained when the initial attacks had been

Contemporary view of the site at which the Battle of Shrewsbury took place in July 1403.

beaten off by the Cheshire archers. Once again, experts dispute the total number of casualties, some suggesting that more than 3,000 men died at Shrewsbury that late summer afternoon.

King Henry is said to have wept over the body of Hotspur, his former friend and ally, and he agreed to his burial at Whitchurch. However to dispel rumours that Hotspur had survived, Henry was later obliged to have his body dug up and displayed in the market square in Shrewsbury before having it beheaded, quartered and displayed in various parts of the country: so much for sentiment. Hotspur's remains were finally given to his widow and were permanently buried in York Minster.

Hotspur's fellow leaders were all hanged, drawn and quartered with the exception of the Earl of Douglas who was ransomed. Henry despatched his army north to confront Hotspur's father, the Earl of Northumberland, who had delayed in coming to his son's assistance because of the Scots threatening the north.

However, battle was avoided and Henry graciously pardoned the Earl. Five years later the Earl of Northumberland again rebelled against Henry and was killed. The Welsh Prince Glyndwr was never fond of pitched battle, preferring to wage a guerrilla war from his Welsh stronghold and he continued to irritate Henry for years to come.

Henry IV died ten years after the Battle of Shrewsbury, wearied and weakened by years of continual confrontation.

One of his legacies is the Church of St Mary Magdalen, Battlefield, which he ordered to be built on the site of the battle to commemorate the dead. It took six years to build and completed in 1409, later restored in the 18th century.

Despite much being known about of the Battle of Shrewsbury, the exact site is still disputed and unverified, defying searches by experts. The ridge north of the church is said to be where the rebels were based but others claim that the heaviest fighting took place a mile to the west of the ridge.

Work in St Mary Magdalen's churchyard has unearthed lots of bones but nothing resembling the mass grave that might be expected. Over the years artefacts such as a poleaxe, iron arrowheads and remnants of metal have also been unearthed.

The BBC series, *Two Men in a Trench,* visited the area in 2001 in an effort to locate the exact site of the Battle of Shrewsbury and despite using metal detectors and unearthing more arrowheads and metal fragments, they too were unable to locate any evidence of a mass grave, despite also excavating in the nearby village of Albright Hussey.

It is possible that St Mary Magdalen church was intended as a permanent memorial to the dead of that terrible day, and therefore might well have been constructed right over the site of the mass grave which would explain why, so far, the battle's burial ground has defied all attempts to find it.

The Battle of Shrewsbury was significant for three reasons:

1. It was the first time that English expertise with the longbow, which had won major battles for the English overseas (Poitiers and Crécy), was used by both sides in an English civil war.

2. The battle was immortalised in William Shakespeare's, *Henry IV Part I,* a largely factual account in which all the major characters were identified apart from Falstaff, who had no part to play at Shrewsbury.

3. The Battle of Shrewsbury was seen by some historians as the first of the series of civil wars to come, the Wars of the Roses, which would finally end eight decades later in 1485.

Today the battle site is surrounded by agricultural land and there is a visitors' route around the site provided by the local authority. Battlefield Church, a viewing mound and a car park enhance the visitor's efforts to re-live the battle in their imagination. They will be standing just off the Shrewsbury by-pass, the A5124, which crosses the southern edge of the battlefield where Henry IV first took up his position.

The Church of St Mary Magdalen at Battlefield is now considered the most probable site of the mass grave containing the 3000 dead from the battle.

ACKNOWLEDGEMENTS

I am indebted to many people and organisations who have helped me in the course of my research and writing. In particular:

Barbara Pym Society – Yvonne Cocking and Eileen Roberts (St. Hilda's College, Oxford)
Battlefield Visitor Centre – Jeremy Jagger (www.battlefield1403.com)
Carding Mill Valley (National Trust Education) – Chris Stratton
Hawkstone Park Hotel and Golf Club – Liz Tiernan (www.hawkstone-park.com)
Ironbridge Gorge Museum Trust – John Powell (www.ironbridge.org.uk)
Llanymynech Golf Club
Market Drayton Visitor Information Centre – Clive Chapman
    (www.shropshiretourism.co.uk/market-drayton)
Margaret Jones (Corvedale Church of England Primary School)
Mary Webb Society – Liz Stamps (marywebb@blueyonder.co.uk)
Michael Symonds (Headmaster, Bedstone College)
Mytton and Mermaid, Atcham – Ann Ditella
    (www.myttonandmermaid.co.uk)
National Trust, Carding Mill Valley – Chris Stratton
    (www.nationaltrust.org.uk)
Nick Britten (*Daily Telegraph*)
Percy Thrower Garden Centre – Andrew Gledhill (www.g-l.co.uk)
Peter Klein (author of *Temptation & Downfall of the Vicar of Stanton Lacy*)
Robin Bebb (Newnes Touring Caravan Park)
Roger Whitehouse
SCMC Archives (www.shropshirecmc.org.uk)
Sharon Walters (*Shropshire Star*)
Shrewsbury Library (www.shropshire.gov.uk/library.nsf)
Shrewsbury Museum Services – Peter Boyd
    (www.shrewsburymuseums.com)
Shrewsbury Abbey – Mike Purslow (www.shrewsburyabbey.com)
Shrewsbury Visitor Information Centre – Robert Elliott
Shropshire Hills Discovery Centre (discovery.centre@shropshire.gov.uk)
Shropshire Mines Trust - Adrian Pearce
    (www.shropshiremines.org.uk)
Shropshire Mining and Caving Club (www.shropshirecmc.org.uk)
Stuart Sue Ellis (Whittington Castle)
Bog Visitor Centre (www.bogcentre.co.uk)

Wenlock Olympian Society – Helen Cromarty
(www.wenlock-olympian-society.org.uk)
Whittington Castle – Sue Ellis
Wrexham & Shropshire Railway – Leanne Tobin
(www.wrexhamandshropshire.co.uk)
Wroxeter Roman City – Nola Ames
(www.english-heritage.org.uk/wroxeter)

The publishers would also like to thank Alistair Coats and Hannah McMillan for their invaluable editorial and design assistance on this book.

USEFUL ADDRESSES

Battlefield 1403 (Visitor Centre)
Battlefield Farm, Upper Battlefield, Shrewsbury SY43 DB
Tel: 01939 210905   www.battlefield1403.com

Bog Visitor Centre
Stiperstones, Shropshire, SY5 0NG
Tel: 01743 792 484   www.bogcentre.co.uk

Bridgnorth Visitor Centre
The Library, Listley Street, Bridgnorth WV16 4AW
Tel: 01746 763257

Church Stretton Visitor Centre
Church Street, Church Stretton, SY6 6DQ
Tel: 01694 723133

Ironbridge Gorge Visitor Centre
Coach Road, Coalbrookdale, Telford, TF8 7DQ
Tel: 01952 435900
www.ironbridge.org.uk

Ludlow Visitor Centre
Castle Square, Ludlow SY8 1AS
Tel: 01584 875053

217

Market Drayton Visitor Centre
49 Cheshire Street, Market Drayton TF9 1PH
Tel: 01630 653114

Much Wenlock Museum and Visitor Centre
The Museum, High Street, Much Wenlock TF13 6HR
Tel: 01952 727679

Oswestry Town Visitor Centre
2 Church Terrace, Oswestry SY11 2TE
Tel: 01691 662488

Shrewsbury Tourist Information
The Visitor Information Centre, Rowley's House
Barker Street, Shrewsbury SY1 1QH
Tel: 01743 281200
www.shropshiretourism.co.uk

Shropshire Hills Discovery Centre
School Road, Craven Arms, Shropshire SY7 9RS
Tel: 0345 678 9024
www.shropshire.gov.uk

Shrewsbury Museum and Art Gallery
Rowley's House Museum, Barker Street, Shrewsbury
Shropshire, SY1 1QH
Tel: 01743 281205
www.shrewsburymuseums.com

Stokesay Castle
Craven Arms, Shropshire SY7 9AH
Tel: 01588 672544

Wroxeter Roman City
Shrewsbury, Shropshire SY5 6PH
Tel: 01743 761330

BIBLIOGRAPHY

Apperley, Charles James, *Memoirs of the Life of the Late John Mytton, Esq. – with Notices of his Hunting, Shooting, Driving, Racing, Eccentric and Extravagant Exploits* (Read Books, 2006).

Battle of Shrewsbury, The (Stephen Maxfield, 2003)

Carr, Rev. E. D., *A Night in the Snow* (London: James Nisbet & Co., 1865).

Colledge, J.J., and Warlow, Ben, *Ships of the Royal Navy: A Complete Record of All Fighting Ships from the 15th Century to the Present* (Newbury: Chatham Publishing, 2006).

Coxill, David, 'Coalbrookdale Coalfield' in *Shrewsbury Caving and Mining Club Journal*, Vol. 3.

Dickins, Gordon, *An Illustrated Literary Guide to Shropshire* (Shropshire: Shropshire Books, 1987).

Harvey, Robert, *Clive: The Life and Death of a British Emperor* (New York: St. Martin's Press, 2000).

Hibberd, Dominic, *Wilfred Owen: A New Biography* (London: Weidenfeld & Nicolson, 2002).

Kirby, Terry, *The Trials of the Baroness* (London: Mandarin, 1991).

Klein, Peter, *The Temptation and Downfall of the Vicar of Stanton Lacy* (Ludlow: Merlin Unwin Books, 2005).

Knight, Steven and Ohlgren, Thomas Ed., *Robin Hood and Other Outlaw Tales* (Michigan, Western Michigan University Medieval, 1997).

Kynaston, John, *Visitation of Shropshire* 1623 (Harleian Society).

Lyle, Sandy, *To the Fairway Born: The Autobiography* (London: Headline Publishing Group, 2006).

Perrett, Bryan *The Battle Book: Crucial Conflicts in History from 1469BC* (Arms & Armour Press)

Phillips, Graham, *The Chalice of Magdalene: The Search for the Cup That Held the Blood of Christ* (Vermont: Bear & Company, 2004).

Salopian Journal, 1839

Sprawson, Charles, *Haunts of the Black Masseur: The Swimmer as Hero* (London: Vintage, 1993).

Trinder, Barrie, *A History of Shropshire* (Stroud: Phillimore and Co., 1998).

Wright, Billy and Butler, Byron, *One Hundred Caps and all that* (Tonbridge: Robert Hale Ltd, 1962).

Yate, Bob, *Shropshire Union Railway: Stafford to Shrewsbury including the Coalport Branch* (Gwent: The Oakwood Press, 2003).

INDEX

220

Index

Also published by Merlin Unwin Books

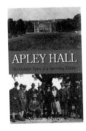